W9-BZR-278

WOKCRAFT

BY CHARLES & VIOLET SCHAFER

ILLUSTRATED BY WIN NG

YERBA BUENA PRESS

SAN FRANCISCO

1972

*To our Chinese friends
who have always enriched and
often ennobled our world with
their philosophy, their humor
and their marvelous cuisine.*

ISBN 0-912738-01-4

Library of Congress Card #73-183774
Printed in The United States Of America
Copyright © 1972 By Yerba Buena Press,
Published by Taylor & Ng • Yerba Buena Press.
400 Valley Drive
Brisbane, California 94005
        All Rights Reserved
        First Edition
        First Yerba Buena Press Printing 1972
        Second Printing 1973
        Third Printing 1974
        Fourth, Fifth & Sixth Printings 1975
        Seventh, Eighth, & Ninth Printings 1976
        Tenth & Eleventh Printings 1977

Dutch Translation, *Chinese Kookkunst.*
published by
Bert Bakker BV, Amsterdam
First Printing, 1975

Distributed by Random House, Inc.
and in Canada By Random House of Canada, Ltd.
ISBN 0-394-70788-5

About the authors

Charles Schafer is a nationally recognized conference consultant and authority on continuing education. As a young man, he went around the world twice and enjoyed two tours of duty in China. He was District Traffic Manager for Pan American World Airways in Hong Kong when it fell to the Japanese.

After World War II, he returned to China at the request of T.V. Soong on special assignment as Assistant to the Business Manager of China National Aviation Corporation. In this capacity he flew to all the major air terminal cities in China in 1946 and 1947.

These Chinese journeys, interspaced with living-in periods, deeply influenced his tastes in food and in home design and decoration. They also affected his cultural interests and the way he courted his wife. He writes of his Chinese era with affection.

Mr. Schafer selected and tested all the *Wokcraft* recipes except for breads and confections. His wife, Violet, who co-authors this book is the author of *Herbcraft* and the sharer of his Chinese friends, his woks and his little house. She tested the steamed and fried breads, dumplings and confections.

Wokcraft brings Illustrator Win Ng into familiar territory. Like the memorable and joyful drawings he did for *Herbcraft,* these reflect a skillful use of research as well as a gifted eye for the Chinese environment observed by a native of San Francisco's Chinatown and traveler in the Orient. They capture the symbolism, reality and unbelievable quality of the East.

Wokcraft illustrations tell again why Mr. Ng's drawings of San Francisco have sold in the thousands and why his "Casual Couple" reproductions have delighted as many. Exciting, often multi-meaning in implication, they are a lively and humorous interpretation of words and ideas. They make *Wokcraft* a continually fresh and provocative picture book that is interesting to all ages and all persuasions.

With L.C. Spaulding Taylor, also a recognized artist, Mr. Ng heads Taylor and Ng, San Francisco's famous pace-setting "Department Store of Handcrafts." It features outstanding work of craftsmen from around the world. In the last two years, the store has evinced deep interest in Oriental cuisine, having a section entirely devoted to Oriental utensils and pots, teas and condiments. Both gentlemen are gourmet cooks.

CONTENTS

A RICH HERITAGE

How much we owe to Chinese culture! How much it adds to the depth and color of living.

My experience in China as a young man, the pleasures of friendships with its people from Peking and Hong Kong to San Francisco, and subtle enslavement to its cuisine profoundly marked my philosophy of the world and homemaking.

The catalyst was the small but intense view I had for two years into a life more mysterious and more spiritually grand than anything I had observed in previous travels in Europe and at home.

My education began one day thirty years ago when I flew into Hong Kong on the China Clipper. I was to be the new manager of Pan American's Far Eastern office.

The first honor was to receive a Chinese name for my calling cards. My Chinese staff cleverly selected characters that would do double duty. They sounded like my American name. More importantly, their meaning captured the essence of my position in terms both flattering and respectful. I became "Beautiful Teacher."

The fact was that I became a happy learner.

The manners, customs, daily encounters, the food taught me how ceremony elevates the simplest human condition to a position of dignity. The sharing of meals demonstrated that eating in China had nothing in the world that compared with it. It was a demonstration of plenty, an expression of shared wealth, a gift offered with both hands, and, like good design, cunningly varied.

Many of the dishes offered to me even at feasts are within your capacity to make. I have proved that — with some help from my wife. So you can believe me when I tell you you can produce Chinese gourmet fare even if you aren't the world's greatest chef and even if you don't have the kitchen nonpareil.

Many dishes you can make with pots and pans you already own. Then you can graduate to using Chinese kitchen utensils just to have the pride and experience of cooking with an authentic Oriental accent. You can be a Wokmaster!

KITCHEN TALK -
ON BECOMING A WOKMASTER

When I had an apartment in Shanghai, key money was $2500 US and up. This outrageous cumshaw opened the door to the living quarters, but not the kitchen. I never saw the kitchen after committing the gaffe of trying to paint it into respectability. The cook scolded me, removed my paint bucket and brush and banished me. This Bluebeard ploy provoked a mad desire to know what went on in this forbidden place.

So began my long search for a Chinese kitchen of my own with recipes to make it come alive.

I hoarded memories of tastes, textures and color combinations. I collected now-yellowing scraps of paper with recipes noted in Chinese and English. I savored the very names of dishes — Green Jade and Red Coral; Phoenix Tail Fish; Eight Jewel Pudding; Chicken Velvet; Golden Moons on a Silver Sea; Duck with Eight Precious Stuffings; Gold Coin and Lion's Head Pork; White Cut Chicken and Ham in Green Paradise; Cloud Swallows; Singing Rice; Dragon's Eyes; Ten Thousand Arrows Piercing the Clouds, and Snow Balls. What a million miles removed this was from meat-and-potatoes style cooking and recipes no more exciting than "Henry's Cookies!"

I saved menus from banquets and pasted them in a big scrapbook. The one I attended for Their Excellencies, Ambassadors Johnson and Gauss in Hong Kong brought a parade of:

Pigeon Eggs and Bird's Nest Soup
Shark's Fin
Roast Chicken, Yunnan Ham
Stewed Wild Pigeon, Fresh Mushrooms
Roast Suckling Pig and Condiments
Vegetables in Cream
Partridge Congee
Rice Melange
Pastry
Fruit

I whet my lips over menus *In a Shantung Garden* — a breakfast of mangoes, ripe lychees, tea, pink-and-white ham, eggplant pancakes and ginger. And who but a Chinese would mask the youthful insipidity of fresh-laid eggs with soy to effect the respectability of age? Who but a Chinese would climax a party with a soup of candied crab apples floating in vintage champagne?

Occasionally I enjoyed a real find like the well used pages of recipes prepared by Chinese ladies in classes at the Peking YWCA.

When I returned home, I married and added my wife's Chinese friends to the sum of my own. They shared recipes with us for the asking and meticulously translated restaurant menus for us.

At times they demonstrated Chinese extravaganzas in their kitchens with us at their elbows. Among them were American missionaries, Chinese artists, doctors, writers, nurses, shopkeepers, airline executives, graduate students, professors and importers.

Usually they cooked from memories of fragrant kitchens in Changsha, Peking, Hong Kong, Shanghai, Canton, Nanking and Singapore. Many had never cooked before coming to the United States.

They became expert out of sheer hunger for food from home. Theirs was a triumph of interpretation and accommodation worthy of the practical genius of the Chinese. They managed to produce heavenly fare with their Chinese style of cooking regardless of the Western equipment and substitute foods and seasonings.

For years before woks were common in our area, we cooked in Chinese with only a big skillet, a Dutch oven Aunt Clara gave us for a wedding present, and some ancient, 60 year old kettles we inherited from May Burling Porter.

The lack of a Chinese kitchen never kept us from enjoying Chinese cook-ins. With their infinite tact, our Chinese friends accepted the inefficiencies of our situation. My wife would say, "I will clean the kitchen *after* we have the party" so they could cook with abandon and never fear to mess up the shining place with flying oil. "Have many bowls," was all they suggested, "and the biggest kettles, frying pans and pots you can find or borrow."

We brought off some great feasts — all of us amateurs — without a Chinese kitchen. So can you.

It is fun, of course, to have the Chinese utensils. They give authority to your role as Chinese chef. And they are readily available.

Now we have a Chinese kitchen. It takes up only 20x22x10½ inches for storage in our small house. This accommodates two woks — a 14-inch wok with steaming racks, collar, and cover nested inside and a 12-inch wok with a handle. Stored with them are a bamboo cleaning brush and a small stainless

oil pot. Everything fits neatly under our built-in oven behind cabinet doors on which we hang our ladles, turner and skimmer. A two-layered bamboo steamer — too handsome to store out of sight — is allowed to dress up the kitchen counter. A drawer next to the oven, and out of reach of small children who visit, has room for two cleavers and several pairs of chopsticks used in cooking.

If our kitchen were not so small, we'd have all our Chinese Kitchen visible and hang the woks and utensils over the stove. The point is, the Chinese Kitchen can fit any size kitchen you may have with very little rearranging.

THE CHINESE KITCHEN

The All-Purpose Wok

Authentic Chinese cookery asks relatively little of you. Like a wok.

My first encounter with this miraculous pan was to consider its spelling.

"Should it be spelled *wauk, kwok, wak, wock, wog* or *wok*?" asked a Chinese friend, pronouncing the word in Chinese. "It sounds like *wauk*, doesn't it?"

We have seen all of these spellings, but most often of late find the word spelled *wok*.

This Chinese classic is a triumph of kitchen engineering. It has had no need for design improvements or changes after centuries and millions of satisfied users. Here you have an ancient, bowl-shaped model that cleverly and economically exploits heat whether you have the ultimate in stoves or only a humble brazier or portable alcohol heater.

Practically universal in its use, it stars as sauce pan, frying pan, deep fryer, sauté pan and braising pan. That is not all it can do: you can use it for steaming, simmering and parboiling. So a wok is not extravagant to own and could well be the ideal gift for a bride and groom. It is certainly not a pan that cooks only in Chinese!

Best of all, it can grow old with you and after many seasons of tempering become worthy of inclusion among your heirlooms.

Buying a Wok

Woks come in stainless steel with copper bottoms, in iron, copper, brass and aluminum. The best — for heating up evenly — are made of rolled, tempered steel. They range in diameter from 12 to 24 inches, the biggest being for restaurants or barbecues.

Our 12 and 14-inch woks are rolled and tempered steel. They can cook enough for company or just for two. They can cook a whole chicken or fry one egg. They can cook a meal for a family or a dish for a bachelor.

Buy big when you buy because you can cook small in a big wok, but you cannot cook big in a small wok.

A ring holder with vents to release heat supports our 14-inch wok over the burner on the stove. This keeps the pan from rolling or tipping in use. A handled cover fits snugly over the wok like a big hat.

Woks on Gas, Electric or Wood-Burning Stoves

We have always preferred to cook with electricity. Despite all fiats from cooks who insist that gas is the only way to cook, we have managed exceedingly well with our steel woks.

Although there is such a thing as a wok range, you don't have to remodel your kitchen to accommodate your wok. In fact, if you are lucky enough to have your grandmother's old wood-burning stove, just remove a lid and set your wok right in over the flames.

Also on the market is a portable alcohol table stove that accommodates a wok. This efficient unit can extend your fixed stove capacity when you need more heating units or it can put wok cookery within reach of small households with minimum facilities.

Wok Character

Like your grandmother's iron skillet, the wok is never washed in harsh soaps or detergents or scoured with steel wool. Technically, it should have only one soap bath — before you begin to use it. Then let it age into a sooty affair and cherish it for its *wok hay* character, not for nasty cleanness.

Seasoning the Wok

Seasoning the wok will keep food from sticking. So, before using it for the first time, wash it thoroughly with soap, dry it completely. Then with several thicknesses of paper toweling saturated with salad oil, rub the inside of the wok to close the pores in the metal. With fresh toweling, keep rubbing the oiled surface until the toweling comes away clean. Put the wok in a 375° oven or place it over high heat on the stove. It is now ready to use.

To clean the wok after each use, rinse with hot water, scrub with a bamboo brush or nylon pad and dry immediately over a burner on the stove. When it cools, rub lightly with oil and store.

Like all cherished possessions, the wok will reward you for taking good care of it. Tempered steel woks will stain and rust if you do not store them clean and completely dry. It is much less of a chore to clean than any other pans we own. The smooth bowl assures that.

Eclectic Performer — An All-Purpose Pot for Every Cuisine

Nearly every dish you make — morning, noon or night — you can prepare in a wok: sauces, soups, stews, deep-fried and steamed foods. Two are nice to have, one for rice and a smaller one for meats and vegetables.

Don't be surprised if two are not enough once you become a Wokmaster. So famous a cook as Craig Claiborne owns ten. "I think they are the most efficient cooking pot that I know," he says. He should know, for as food editor of the New York *Times,* he cooked in many styles besides Chinese.

If it is your fate to have only one pan for the nonce, hope it is a wok like the one we saw hanging in a rustic cabin in the New Mexico mountains. The mistress of the simple house pointed to it as the most useful gift that ever came her way "except for a gift box of seeds to plant a field with herbs, flowers and vegetables."

WOK KITCHEN COMPANIONS

Cleavers

We consider these wickedly sharp choppers a necessary luxury. They come in two weights — light for slicing soft meats and vegetables; heavy, for chopping bones, disjointing fowl and reducing garlic cloves and fresh ginger to pulp with its blade.

Accept them for what they are — not shining blades, but tempered steel that stains and ages but keeps a superb edge.

We feel lucky to have some big old steel knives from the cook's shack of Colorado's Silver King Mine which my father managed in the early years of this century. The cook so prized one of them that he engraved his name and town of origin on the blade. Somehow my mother came into possession of these knives and for fifty years cherished their sharpness. Finally they came to us with their ancient stains intact to become compatible companions for our Chinese cleavers.

Keep your cleavers clean, wipe them perfectly dry after using, store them out of reach of children, and let them age gracefully. From time to time, have a professional sharpen them for you or use a fine grain whetstone to touch them up occasionally.

Cleavers will chop fine or coarse. Their design, weight and balance give you more control over the slicing process than possible with ordinary knives.

They are addictive! With a little practice, you will achieve an authority and mastery that will make you disdain other once favorite knives. You will never want to use anything else for chopping. And what other tool has a blade broad enough to carry choppings to the wok or heavy enough to mash a garlic clove with a single blow?

Chopping Block

The Chinese use a section of tree trunk about six inches high and 18 inches in diameter. We make do with a breadboard.

Oil Pot

We have a chrome oil pot with a spout hardly bigger than a bird's beak. It holds a cupful of peanut oil. It is designed to release only the necklace of oil you need for stirfrying. It is a handsome accessory in the Chinese Kitchen.

Brass Wire Skimmer

This decorative piece with its bamboo handle comes in handy when you are deep frying or boiling. Use it to skim particles of food from the oil before they burn and prevent your using the oil a second time.

Forged Iron Ladles and Turner

These have long, 16-inch handles ending in wooden holders to prevent heat building up. The blade of the turner curves to the shape of the wok. You can use ladle and turner during stirfrying much as a salad tosser works with fork and spoon. The iron rusts if you do not wipe these tools clean and dry after each use.

Bamboo Brush

This handsome bundle of stiff split bamboo serves to scrub the cooking surface of the wok and clean it after cooking. It fits the fist naturally for a vigorous rolling action. It is not a "crumb duster" to "give iced cakes a perfect, professional look by brushing off excess crumbs," as claimed by a feature writer in a Los Angeles newspaper! Use the brush that way if you like, but don't say we didn't warn you. The bamboo is tough and would probably remove a few things besides crumbs the way my wife once did. She squared off to blow out candles on her birthday cake. In one mighty effort, she not only managed that but also blew off all the chopped walnuts the hostess had lightly sprinkled on.

Chopsticks

You will find bamboo chopsticks as versatile as the wok. With them you can sort and fish things out of the wok without burning your hands. You can beat eggs with them. You can stir and whip. They do not heat up or break. They are ideal for shaking off surplus oil when you are deep frying. We have also seen a Chinese cook use one as a thermometer for deep frying. She held the chopstick in the heating oil. As soon as bubbles began to stream into the oil from the end of the chopstick, she said the oil was hot enough for deep frying. They are easy to clean and require minimum storage space.

Chopsticks as Tableware

Chopsticks vary in length from 9½ to 11½ inches. Some are round, some square. They are made of gold, ivory, lacquered wood, coral, bamboo, bone, ebony and, alas, plastic. There are many refinements in surface design. We have silver ones that simulate bamboo.

To use them instead of Western flatware in eating Chinese food makes it possible to bring food to your mouth with just the right amount of sauce coating each morsel. Spoons and forks scoop up too much sauce and coarsen the taste.

If you fear to be inexpert, you can find many books that explain in words and pictures how to use these "quick little boys." Forge ahead bravely with the knowledge that many Chinese admit to being amateurs with chopsticks all their lives.

"I do not hold the chopsticks the way the books tell you to," says a Chinese friend. And she uses chopsticks every day of her life to eat her meals.

So, to each his own! If you manage well enough to satisfy your hunger, you must be doing something right with your chopsticks no matter how you hold them.

Porcelain Spoons

These are nice to have. They do not heat up like silver soup spoons. And they do ornament a table setting whether they are plain white or decorated.

Bamboo Steamer

The Chinese cook can get along without an oven but never without a steamer. This is not the same as making do with a double boiler, however. The Chinese have bamboo, lantern-shaped steamers. There have been some misconceptions about this ingenious kitchen accessory. Although it looks like a handy tote or storage bin, it is actually an assemblage of ring layers. These rings and the lid are all purchased separately. By stacking these layers over water in your wok you can steam a number of dishes simultaneously with one heat source and the same water. It is good to have the bamboo lid be-

cause it minimizes condensation. If you do not buy one, and use your wok lid instead, place waxed paper or foil over the food being steamed.

These stacked steamers come in sizes from 8 inches in diameter to 24 inches. For home use, 10-inchers are usual.

The usefulness of some method of steaming is not to be underestimated because steaming is the best method of reheating foods.

Do-it-yourself alternatives to the bamboo steamer are many. You can place cake racks in the bottom of the wok to support dishes or punch holes in an empty coffee can and use that for a support. For wet steaming, all you need is a pot big enough to hold the bowl that holds the food and a good cover on top.

Retriever for Steamed Dishes

This three-pronged metal gadget is a safety device as anyone who has steamed foods will appreciate. Steam burns are vicious. Shop for this item as prices vary sharply.

Kitchen God

A dashing addition to any kitchen about to be Sinologized is a kitchen god. It is probably heresy, but our kitchen god is a small bronze Buddha in lotus position facing the stove from an elevated ledge. Like the silver chopsticks, it was brought as a gift to the little house by an old friend from Hong Kong. You may prefer a more orthodox print or painting of the kitchen god suitably framed in happiness red.

GETTING READY TO PERFORM

To come off as a virtuoso-Wokmaster requires a little something extra from you besides being a careful shopper/chopper. It will help if you are a combination of Sherlock Holmes, Richard Halliburton and the Mad Scientist. And when you approach recipes you think are especially difficult, sing lustily, talk merrily and dance a jig. Never despair if the recipe calls for two eggs and all you have is one goose egg and one hen egg. Crack them and get on with the cooking, confident of success.

As Good for Taste Buds as for Health!

What a reward is in store for you! You will master a cuisine filled with nuances of texture and flavor equal to any in the world. You will prepare tasty dishes for pennies when you like. As you dine on your own cooking, you may deduce the secrets of the ageless Chinese. You will bring to your table a nutritious diet worthy of a professional.

The pleasure of eating in Chinese should be much enhanced for the knowing that the Chinese diet is good for you and may be regarded as health food. The Chinese, in fact, are perpetually on a diet — eating more vegetables than animal foods, more greens than starch and few sweets. Fats appear more as cooking material than as eating stuff. The ratio is for more mineral, vitamin and bulk content than for calories. Stirfrying leaves the nourishment of food least affected. Oil is not the important ingredient. So, let the inventive genius of the Chinese cooks rub off on you, for cooking in Chinese is a good "way."

What follows relates almost entirely to what you can produce with a wok. You do not have to be an expert to prepare these dishes.

USING THE CLEAVERS AND THE CHOPPING BLOCK

Time spent in careful selection of fresh meats, fish, poultry and vegetables is necessary prologue to time spent in the kitchen. There, you will spend most of your time preparing food and the least time cooking it.

Your shopping is done, the vegetables and meats are clean and ready to chop. Your kitchen and work areas are clean and uncluttered. Everything you need to work with is laid out and within arm's reach.

Preparation — Philosophy and Techniques

The Chinese reserve the magic of cutlery for the privacy of the kitchen. This custom spares guests the struggle of cutting and chopping foods at the table. What a graceful arrangement to have the cook do all the chopping and let guests simply enjoy the tastes, aromas, textures and colors of dishes set before them!

Recipes dictate what you do with the cleaver:
Slice straight across the grain: meats, mushrooms, scallions, leafy vegetables
Slice diagonally: celery, anise, Chinese cabbage
Dice
Chop fine or mince
Shred into strips
It may take time to get used to the cleaver for chopping. But stick with it until you produce uniform pieces. This assures a good looking dish and, more important, uniform cooking. Few menus require more than an hour of preparation.

USING THE WOK

Although there are at least 120 Chinese characters to describe cooking processes, you can limit your maiden efforts to three — stirfrying, boiling and steaming. Deep frying is a fourth method you will want to try in the wok if, for one thing, you want to prepare nuts as only the Chinese can and excel at other "little hearts."

Many recipes that follow are stirfries. Some are steamed. All have been tested in a steel wok.

A Word About Seasonings

You will find no salt and pepper on the Chinese table. These seasonings and others concern the cook during food preparation and cooking processes. The cook introduces seasonings in marinades and glazes and adds them to oil heating in the wok for stirfries. The reason for this is simple: the cook wants to bring out some natural flavors or suppress others. Chinese seasoning is subtle. It does not mask or overwhelm.

Stirfrying

Invite your muse and start with an orderly kitchen. You would never believe the chaos that can ensue if the breakfast dishes aren't done before you start cooking in Chinese.

Always start with a clean, dry wok. Bring it to high heat, directly over the burner if you are using a wok with a wooden handle and can lift it off the burner to control the temperature as you work. Or seat the wok in a collar over the burner if you are using a two-handled wok.

When the wok is hot, ring the upper edge of its bowl with a necklace of oil. The "big fire" under the wok may look as though it will burn everything you are working on. It won't. Just keep things stirred and tossed with your turner until things are just done — a matter of a few minutes. Once you have made a dish a few times you will have a feel for it. You can start improvising and experimenting and keeping your eye on the food instead of the clock.

Try a Recipe or Two

Here are two simple recipes that call stirfry principles into play.

HOT LETTUCE

This is not bank language for stolen greenbacks. It describes a dish that is often the first vegetable stirfry a Chinese girl makes when she is learning to cook in her mother's kitchen. With it she gets her first lesson in marrying seasonings with the oil before stirring in the vegetables. It is simple, delicious and typically Chinese. For a start, make this half recipe.

1 tablespoon light salad oil
Sprinkling of salt and pepper
Small piece of garlic
½ head of iceberg lettuce
1 tablespoon oyster sauce thinned with sherry

Break lettuce into pieces with your hands as you would for a salad. Pat lettuce dry with a clean towel so it won't spit at you when you toss it into the wok.

Heat oil in wok. Add salt, pepper and garlic. Stir quickly and remove garlic. Add lettuce. Use your turner to keep lettuce moving briskly. This should take only two minutes. Add oyster sauce, stir and cover. Cook one minute. Serve at once. The lettuce should retain its fresh greenness and crispness.

BEEF WITH CELERY

After stirfrying this dish, you may never want celery prepared any other way. You can invent numerous other stirfries to your taste and rescue good, green vegetables from washed out mediocrity.

½ pound tender lean beef
1 tablespoon cornstarch in 1 tablespoon soy
2 cups sliced celery
3 tablespoons oil
½ teaspoon salt in 1/3 cup water or soup stock
2 oz. can mushroom pieces

Slice beef in narrow strips, place in bowl and
stir in cornstarch and soy mixture. Set aside.

Thinly slice celery on the diagonal. Set aside.

Heat oil in wok over big fire. Stirfry beef until
browned. Remove and add celery. Toss briefly,
pour in water, salt and mushrooms and cover
wok, stirring now and then. After four minutes,
return beef to wok. Continue cooking with
cover off. As soon as meat is hot, dish is ready.
Serve at once.

Planning Ahead

If you have put *Beef with Celery* on your table
for the first time without having a nervous break-
down, congratulations! You qualify as a well organized soul who foresees what a process requires.

If you are like us, however, you learn from wild
experience. Your kitchen echoes with groans of
"Where is the blankety-blank-blank?" and cries of
"Get me some water!" and "Hurry!"

To cook in Chinese calmly requires this: Arrange
in the order of their use:

Chopped ingredients in bowls

Sauces, seasonings and liquids measured in cups

Put all within easy reach of your wok before
you oil it for your performance. And remember to
place the serving bowls handy, too.

You will quickly gain confidence in the method
and easily combine and cook ingredients simultaneously.

Beautiful Integration

Chinese dishes have a very happy way of joining
the menu. Many times we prepare vegetables and
meats in the Chinese way and serve them with
dishes we fancy from Armenia, Italy, Greece,
France, Norway and Wisconsin! Chinese style vegetables put almost all others to shame. Anyone
who has endured the diced-carrots-and-peas syn-
drome will pin a medal on you for serving stirfried
Beef with Celery. Try it!

EATING CHINESE STYLE —
MENUS AND MANNERS

Very few Chinese recipes provide complete meals in one dish. Rather, the Chinese offer a variety of dishes without repeating tastes and textures. In one meal you may have seafoods, meats, poultry, vegetables and rice. The basic four are 1 meat, 1 fish, 1 vegetable and 1 soup.

The idea is to titillate the palate — to balance dishes — a dry one with a soup; crunchiness with smoothness; big things with miniatures; pungence with sweetness. To avoid repeating tastes requires skill and experience.

The number at table determines the number of dishes to be prepared. For practical purposes, this means 2 dishes for 2 people; 3 or 4 dishes for 3 or 4. As the number at table increases, preparations become complicated. For more than 8, the cook makes elaborate efforts.

Chinese banquets are multiples of 8 dishes. James Reston of the New York *Times* reported his bout with an elaborate dinner prepared in his honor during his talks in Peking with Premier Chou En-Lai. For a total of 9 guests a never-ending stream of dishes arrived:

Hors d'oeuvres of prawns, green beans, cold
    duck and chicken; delicious morsels of fish
Oyster broth with tiny oysters the size of a
    quarter and floating slices of cucumber
Shrimp balls, quails' eggs, cabbage and sea slugs
Sweet red wine and an explosive schnapps
    called Mao Tai "which Chou En-Lai used to
    propose a toast, without swallowing a drop."
Mini-dumplings with meat
White bread and butter (!)
Ground pork in lotus leaves (which you do not
    eat)
Corn and bean soup

Sweet Soup
Tangerine tarts, bananas and small triangular
    slices of watermelon

Dinner began at 10 p.m. and ended shortly after midnight. There was much talk. "It was quite a night," said Mr. Reston.

Dining at Home

The Chinese table setting is simple — a pair of chopsticks, a bowl for soup and rice, a porcelain spoon, a tea cup without a handle, no tablecloth. Serving dishes are placed in the center of a round table. Sometimes tables have Lazy Susans because no one passes the food.

To be polite, defer priority to your elders for the opening minutes of the meal. After that, everyone helps himself with his chopsticks. The whole meal is on the table. The cook has told all. You can gauge your appetite.

Tea is served all during the meal.

Stocking Your Larder

The practice of Chinese cookery is a confusing plunge into linguistics at times. The simple listing of ingredients boggles your mind with the possibilities. Hunting down the ingredients on your shopping list becomes an imaginative exercise in accommodation between a variety of Chinese dialects for a single ingredient and an English equivalent.

On a recent shopping trip, we spent 45 minutes in a Chinese supermarket reading our shopping list and comparing items on it with labels on cans, bottles and packages. When we couldn't tell what we were looking at, it did no good to ask the check out clerk.

We finally went home with two big sacks bulging with bean curd, gingko nuts, cloud ears, rock sugar, dried tangerine peel, lotus root, oyster sauce, sesame oil, dried mushrooms, sausage, hoisin sauce, brown bean sauce, plum sauce, star anise (beautiful stuff!), tiger lily buds, water chestnuts and Five Heavenly Spice Powder. The bill was $10.

The big ticket item, the price of which was not visible either on the shelf or the bottle, was the imported rice wine — $2.35 for 5/8 pint. True, it is 46 proof and has a good sweet taste, but gin or sherry will do as well and cost less.

Many of the purchases will be staples on our Chinese shelf for months and serve for many recipes. Had we been concerned with the minimum, we could have made do with sesame oil, soy, peanut oil, plum sauce and possibly oyster sauce — and with other things on our shelves like long-grain rice, cornstarch and wine, we could have cooked in Chinese.

Among *Wokcraft* recipes you will find some exotics that affect the taste of the dish. You will want to test and taste them and decide yourself how much or how little to use and even whether to use them at all once you have tried them.

Using or not using them will not make or destroy you as a Chinese cook. But they will give you an extra that is typically on kitchen shelves in Chinese-American homes.

As you plan to use a recipe, you can decide to get the unusual spice, sauce or ingredient the dish calls for.

The shopping list that follows, with brief commentaries in some cases, includes basic ingredients used in *Wokcraft* recipes. The list shows which are unique and which admit to substitutes. Although many Chinese cook books make frequent use of monosodium glutamate, we have dropped it from our recipes because of recent unfavorable findings by food research scientists.

WOKCRAFT GROCERY LIST

Anise Seeds Aromatic herb seed commonly used in Western cookery.
Substitute Anise extract

Anise, Star Hard, star-shaped "flowers" or cloves about ½ inch in diameter. Imports from China often include broken pieces. Distinctive licorice/anise flavor. Tie in cheesecloth for easy removal from cooking pots. Use with meat, fish and poultry. When ground, 3 or 4 stars produce taste equivalent of ½ teaspoon powdered anise.
Substitute None

Bamboo Shoots Crisp, chewy vegetable that adds texture to dishes. Of hundreds of varieties, only three Japanese varieties are edible. These must be harvested at just the right time during a 10-day period. Chinese and Japanese varieties differ in taste and some claim the Japanese are best. To soften them, shoots are boiled in water used for washing rice. This accounts for white coating on bamboo found in some cans. Rinse off before using.
Substitutes Kohlrabi, celery heart, young cabbage and jicama.

If Pansy Pandora Penelope Phillips hadn't come calling one day with figs from her tree, a package of sharp cheddar and a half piece of jicama for hors d'oeuvres, we would never had discovered what a great substitute jicama is for bamboo shoots.

This Mexican root vegetable resembles a giant rutabaga. It has a thin, hard skin; white, crisp, juicy and slightly sweet meat. It can be eaten raw or cooked and retains its chewiness when cooked. It is now widely available in Western markets and grows as far south as Argentina. It is sometimes called a *yam bean*.

Bean Curd or Cake, Fresh This creamy, bland custard of pureed soybeans is as important and versatile in Chinese cooking as gelatin is in Western cooking. It comes in cakes about 2½ inches square and ½ inch thick. It can be cooked quickly, boiled, steamed, stirfried and even deepfried. Easily digestible, it can be eaten as is. Fresh bean cake is sold packed in water, often refrigerated. It is also sold fried in cubes and blocks.

As the Chinese discovered long ago, soybeans are the vegetarian's best friend. Soybean protein contains all essential amino acids and is the richest natural source of lecithin, good for nerves and necessary for reproduction of new cells. Nutritionists and health food devotees hail the bean as the only vegetable that contains a complete protein that can actually take the place of meat.

Substitute None

Bean Curd, Pickled Made of fermented, boiled soybeans and crushed rice or barley, these cakes have a strong, salty and pungent taste reminiscent of caviar. Sold in jars or cans in semi-liquid form, it is a ready-to-eat seasoning for vegetables, noodle dishes, etc. It is also served as a side dish with pickles and salted peanuts.

Substitute None

Bean Paste, Red This sweet bean paste is used to fill moon cakes, dumplings and to make sweet dishes. You can make it at home. Mash cooked red soybeans, add sugar and fry and dry out in a wok until the ingredients reach a consistency the Chinese describe as "sand." Also available on the market in cans.

Substitute Coconut, chopped dates

Bean Sauce, Brown A fermented thick spicy paste made from yellow soybeans, flour and salt, it adds salty flavor to fish, meats, poultry and vegetables. It is available in cans and jars. Some people prefer Japanese soybean paste called *miso* which can be refrigerated in a covered jar for weeks.

Substitute Bovril

Bean Sauce, Black Use this fermented black soybean paste sparingly because it is potent. Black beans are considered one of major Chinese condiments along with ginger and soy. Sauce dominates fishy taste of fish and is added to meat and poultry. Available in cans. You can also buy salted black beans in plastic bags. They must be soaked before use. When mashed with garlic to form a paste, beans should be fried a little in oil to bring out their taste.

Substitute None

Bean Sprouts The sprouts of mung beans, these small, white easy-to-grow vegetables add texture and succulence to many dishes. They are available in many supermarket vegetable sections, both loose and bagged. They can also be purchased in cans.

Substitutes Shredded onions, parboiled string beans

Cabbage, Chinese or Celery Sometimes known as long cabbage and botanically as *Brassica pekinensis,* it is not to be confused with bok-choy. It is a cylinder of closely fitted, crinkly leaves a foot or more long and 4–6 inches in diameter. It is more refined and delicately tart than common cabbage and is heartier than lettuce. The whole plant is edible. Only the coarse green outer leaves need be boiled. Inner leaves are white, crisp and tender. Inner ribs of leaves are wider than celery and can be eaten raw or cooked like celery. A favored ingredient of soups, stirfries and cabbage rolls.

Substitutes Savoy cabbage, lettuce, celery and spinach

Bok-Choy known botanically as *Brassica chinensis,* is a popular, piquantly delicate vegetable. Its heavier celerylike long smooth white stems widen into crinkly dark green leaves. Center stalks are tipped with yellow flowerets. Often used in combination with meats, poultry and seafood stirfries and added to soups at last minute.

Substitute Romaine lettuce

Cabbage, Pickled Chopped mustard greens packed in brine and fermented or pickled in various ways to add salty flavor and color to all types of dishes including soups.

Substitute Sauerkraut

Chestnuts, Water This water caltrop is a thin-skinned, dark brown, narcissuslike bulb with a white, nutlike center. It adds sweetness and chewiness to many dishes and fillings. Fresh ones are preferred as being sweeter and crisper than canned ones.

Substitutes Jicama or Jerusalem Artichoke

Cloud Ears (Wood or tree fungus) Sold dried, these 1-inch, dark brown fungi double their original size when soaked for 30 minutes. They then assume their fluffy cloud or ear shape. Highly nutritious, they have a tender taste that adds a dimension to stirfried, steamed and braised dishes and soups. No other ingredient approaches them. Often used in same dish with lily buds.

Substitute None

Dragon's Eyes (Longans) Walnut size fruit with white translucent meat and large pit. Delicate and exotic in taste, they are related to but smaller than litchis. Canned longans come peeled, pitted or unpitted, in light syrup. Use in desserts and as unusual accent in sweet sour and other sweet dishes.

Substitutes White seedless grapes or canned litchis

Five Spices Often called "Five Heavenly Spices" powder. We have found more than one version of this finely ground powder. One listed 5 ingredients on the label: cinnamon, cloves, star anise, Szechuan pepper and fennel. Another listed aniseed, cinnamon, licorice, cloves, ginger and nutmeg. The powder lends a delicate but distinctively Oriental aroma and pungence to meat, poultry and nuts. Available in packages in many gourmet shops.

Substitute Allspice

Ginger Root, Fresh Knotted, fibrous, pungent and aromatic, ginger root is a basic seasoning, a screen against fishy odors, and a flavor booster for soups, poultry, meats, vegetables and desserts. Thin slices are added as oil heats in the wok for stirfries and removed much as garlic cloves are before other ingredients are added. Available by weight in vegetable sections of supermarkets. Freezes well.

Substitute Preserved ginger

Ham, Chinese A dark red, well-aged ham used principally to impart flavor and aroma and to garnish. Available in Chinese markets by the pound. All recipes in *Wokcraft* calling for ham intend only Chinese ham or its substitutes.

Substitutes Smithfield, Westphalian hams or Italian prosciutto. At least a 2-year-old ham, and the redder, the better.

Hoisin Sauce Thick, reddish brown and made from soybeans, spices, garlic and chili, hoisin sauce adds a sharp, spicy but slightly sweet flavor to seafoods, meats and poultry. Use carefully, erring on the side of too little rather than too much.

Substitute None

Jujube Although it bears no resemblance to the date palm, it is called the red date because of its soft red skin, datelike pit and sweet date/apple taste. The jujube has been cultivated in China for at least 4,000 years. Oval, 1½–2 inches long, the fruit is from a semi-tropical tree. Available dried like prunes, it assumes its plump original size when cooked. Much treasured for use in jams, sweet dishes and for its bright red presence in sweet soups.

Substitutes Dried prunes or dates

Lily Buds (Golden Needles) Pale gold, these dried, 2–3 inch long tiger lily buds are succulent and highly nutritious. They are cooked with fish, poultry and pork and used in soup, often in combination with cloud ears. After soaking them 30 minutes to 1 hour, rinse and break off tough bud ends and tie in single overhand knot before adding to soups. This makes them more attractive and easier to manage.

Substitute None

Lotus Seeds Dried water lily seeds, these are shaped like dried corn kernels and have a delicate nutty taste. Blanch before using in soups, etc. Pureed and sweetened, they make fillings for moon cakes.

Substitute Blanched almonds

Lotus Root Long, brown tuberous root of the water lily varying from 2–3 inches in diameter and 4–6 inches long. Sold fresh by the piece, canned or dried, each having a different texture and taste. Fresh roots are most desirable. They taste sweeter than potatoes and have a crisp, chewy texture and white perforated meat. Sliced thin and deep fried, lotus root provides an appetizer like a potato chip. Use in soups, stirfried as vegetable, and in sweet dishes.

Substitute None

Melon, Winter These light blue-green melons sold in Chinese markets are larger than our watermelons, usually, and have a snow white, porous meat, 2–3 inches thick beneath the thin hard rind. Available in sections by the pound. After removing seeds and rind, use meat thinly sliced or cut in chunks for soups or pickles. It can also be stirfried as a vegetable. Needs very little cooking.

Substitutes Cucumber, zucchini

Mushrooms, Chinese Dried These vary in size from ½ inch to 2 inches across. Brownish black, they have a distinctive taste. To use, soak in lukewarm water until centers are soft to touch — about 15 minutes. Before using, squeeze dry and remove stems. Straw mushrooms, available canned or dried, are more expensive and even more succulent. They are shaped like closed umbrellas about 1–1½ inches tall.

Substitutes Dried Italian mushrooms. Although nothing is quite like the Chinese dried mushroom, there is nothing to say you can't use any mushrooms you like or can get.

Nuts Raw peanuts, cashews, walnuts, almonds and pinon nuts are all readily available in health food stores.

Oyster Sauce A thick brownish liquid made from oysters, soy sauce and brine, it is usually thinned for use with sherry, soy or water. As a cooking sauce or dip, use in small amounts to add rich, smooth and somewhat salty flavor to dishes. Sold in bottles and cans.
Substitute None

Parsley, Chinese The tender, flat, inch-wide serrated leaves and willowy stems of Chinese parsley have a piquancy and aroma far different from parsley you see in the market every day. Use it sparingly as a garnish or seasoning, for it can easily dominate a dish.
Substitute Cilantro, fresh coriander, watercress

Peanut Oil Clear, amber, tasteless and odorless cooking oil made from peanuts. Imparts a subtle flavor and can be heated to high temperature without smoking. It can be used again and again as it absorbs practically no food odors from cooking ingredients. We use a paper coffee filter to strain oil after each deepfrying and it works very well. Peanut oil turns cloudy at low temperatures without affecting flavor. One Chinese chef points out that fats and oils that do smoke at low temperatures soak into food and lend unpleasant odors and tastes.
Substitutes Vegetable oils but NOT butter, olive oil or shortening

Peas, Snow Chinese pea pods are smaller than garden peas we know. They are flat, have fewer peas inside, but that makes no difference since you eat pod and all with ends and strings removed. Snow peas are treasured for their crisp, tender sweetness. Available fresh in some markets by the pound or fresh frozen, often with water chestnuts included. A green joy on a white dish!
  Substitute Really none, though freshly shelled peas may console you!

Pepper, Chinese Red These aromatic pepper flakes are *hot* and especially recommended to mask fishy tastes.
  Substitute Tabasco

Pepper, Szechwan *(Xanthoxylum piperitum)* Like our black peppercorns, this pepper is mildly hot, pungent and aromatic. It has a small seed used to cook meat and poultry and to make a pepper and salt mix.
  Substitute Peppercorns

Pepper, White This pepper is hot without aroma. It is possible to make a salt and pepper mix and have it ready to use in cooking. Simply heat ¼ cup salt and 2 teaspoons white pepper in a skillet and mix over moderate heat for 5 minutes. Cool and store. Use to season fried squab, shrimp balls, roasts and broiled meat.

Plum Sauce This delicious, sweet/hot, chutneylike sauce made of plums, apricots, chili, vinegar and sugar is a thick golden jam and a favorite with almost all who try it. Superb with hot or cold meats and poultry. It is traditionally served with Peking Duck. It is hard to duplicate the subtle blend, but try our recipe any way: (We used wild plums from our own tree.)

4 pounds fresh plums pitted
1 quart cider vinegar
2 cups brown sugar
1 cup white sugar
2 knobs minced fresh ginger
3 tablespoons salt
½ package mustard seed
2 tablespoons canned green chili peppers
2 tablespoons red canned pimientos
1 small chopped onion
1 clove minced garlic

Cook plums until soft in half the vinegar. Make syrup with other half and sugar in second kettle. Cook until syrupy and add all other ingredients. Bring to boil, reduce heat to simmer and cook until sauce is thick — about 1½ hours.
  Yield: 6–8 ½ pint jars

Rice Flour, Glutinous Made from glutinous rice for use in pastries and sweet dishes.
  Substitute None

Rice Wine There are many varieties, all with far higher volume of alcohol than other wines. For this reason, suggested substitutes are strong, though sherry and other wines will do. Most rice wines are clear or slightly yellow. They range up to 96 proof.
  Substitutes Gin, vodka, brandy

Sausage, Chinese Red and white ½-inch round and 8–9 inches long, these sausages are linked in pairs and sold in plastic packages. Sweet and flavorsome, they are made with pork, pork fat, pork liver, sugar, soy sauce, soybeans, water, salt and grain alcohol. They add rich smoky flavor to steamed and stir-fried dishes.
  Substitute Italian prosciutto

Sesame Oil Expensive, golden oil made from toasted sesame seeds, it is highly fragrant and has an appetizing, nutlike taste. It is used sparingly to flavor soups, fish, poultry and cold dishes. One or 2 drops are sufficient, for the concentrated essence has power. So it isn't really expensive in the long run. It is never used as a cooking oil. It is one of the great oil crops of the world and of great antiquity in India.
Substitute None

Sesame Seeds These small flat white or black seeds are 45–55% oil. Used in sweet cookies, cakes, candies and as seasoning in hot and cold dishes.
Substitute None

Soy Sauce Orientals long ago discovered that soy sauce changes character and reacts differently with each kind of food. In small quantities it enhances natural flavors subtly. In larger quantities, it tends to blend with food. These characteristics explain why it is used without monotony. The tangy, salty brown liquid is made from fermented and pasteurized soybeans, toasted wheat or wheat flour, yeast and salt. There are many types and grades imported from China and Japan. Color ranges from dark to light and in density from thin to thick. The thicker variety is made with molasses. Japanese soy sauce is sweeter, less salty and most widely available.
Substitute Worcestershire sauce, perhaps

Sugar, Rock and Slab Rock sugar comes in yellowish white crystalline lumps as big as your thumb. Use to sweeten tea, soup and glazes. Slab sugar comes in dark brown, rock-hard slabs measuring about ½x3x5 inches. This sugar has a delightful flavor, being made of brown and white sugar and honey. Use a meat pounder to break it up.
Substitutes None

Tea, Litchi All teas are of great antiquity in the Orient. Tea drinking was apparently preceded by the direct chewing of tea leaves to relieve fatigue. Litchi tea is a slightly sweet oolong or black tea scented with yellow blossoms of the litchi. It is one of many fine teas served with meals.
Substitute None

Vinegar, Rice Wine There are red, white and black vinegars. Red is used as a dip for crab and oily dishes; black with braised dishes and as a table condiment; white with sweet-sour dishes. American white vinegar is similar and can be used as an all-purpose substitute. Japanese white wine vinegars are lighter and milder and available in gourmet sections of markets.
Substitutes White wine vinegar, cider vinegar

LITTLE HEARTS, PEANUTS & DUCK'S FEET

In Hong Kong, a friend and I jointly owned a Teak Lady. We put her in the care of a boatmaster at Ah King's Slipway.

Right after work we often had sailing parties and loaded a cargo of tea, beer and "little hearts" to feast the inner man.

Our sail began in a series of near collisions. A myriad of craft tested us as sailors — flotillas of junks taking cargo off steamers at almost 40 buoys in the center of the bay; sampans and seagoing craft with red, tattered sails crossing every which way; Star ferries churning a constant shuttle between Hong Kong and Kowloon.

As we neared Kai Tak Airport, the sea breeze died down and we dropped anchor among scores of other pleasure craft. Inevitably a song fest began and we joined in. Someone always had a guitar and our songs rose and fell over the waters.

"Little Hearts"—The Meal That Went to Sea in a Box

Pleasantly tired at last, we concentrated on the "little hearts" — the finger foods we had ordered from a restaurant early in the day. Among the delectables were sliced duck livers, chicken giblets, cloud swallows and assorted stuffed dumplings. We dined handsomely.

Then tired and happy we caught the offshore wind and sailed home to a harbor, its lights ringing the shores and hanging a delicate necklace on the Peak.

Traveling Smörgasbord

On other occasions we enjoyed little hearts, too. Certain restaurants specialized in them at noontime. First, waiters served tea, then plied us with tray after tray of little hearts for our personal selection.

There was no menu, just a parade of plates. When we finally pushed ourselves back from the table, the waiter counted the empty dishes, computed the charge in his head and we paid on our way out.

A Surprise Inside!

The little hearts I favored most were steamed buns — *bao*. They amazed me and the surprise inside was always a delight.

Who would think these pearly little mounds on a square of paper were bread? Who would guess these crustless, faintly-sweet morsels would be stuffed?

Inside was, indeed, a variety of chopped meats or seafoods with onions, seeds, dried fruits or nuts in a delicious paste. A tablespoon of the hidden filling flavored every bite of bao.

There were both salty and sweet fillings. The only clue to this secret inside was a red dot of food coloring on top of the sweet buns.

Enough for a Thousand and One Nights!

There are thousands of varieties of these Chinese tidbits that "touch the heart." As snacks of great imagination and immensely satisfying character, they rate frequent appearance as hors d'oeuvres and appetizers at your parties. Some are a bit complicated to make but can be made in advance and frozen until you want to use them. Others are so simple and so delicious, don't wait to try them.

CHINESE BREADS – DEEP FRIED, STEAMED AND BOILED

DEEP FRIED PORK BALLS

These delicious pork tidbits are belted with fresh dough. Three simple steps do the job. Since the meat balls are on the dry side, you may want to go one step farther and devise a warm dipping sauce to your own taste.

Dough
> 1 cup unbleached flour
> ½ teaspoon salt
> 1 egg yolk (Save egg white to secure
>   dough belts)
> 3 tablespoons warm water

Sift flour with salt. Stir in egg yolk and warm water. Knead until smooth. If you find the dough is difficult to work, simply wet your hands under the faucet with warm water and continue knead-

ing. This is a pleasant business since the dough is wholesomely fragrant. You will end with a ball the size of a tennis ball. Wrap it in waxed paper and set aside. You can make this dough well ahead if you like and hold it in the refrigerator until ready for use.

Filling:
> Mix
> 2 cups finely minced pork
>   (The Chinese don't remove all fat.
>   This assures a smooth mix.)
> 2 minced green onions
> 1 beaten egg
> 1 tablespoon soy
> 1 teaspoon corn starch
> Salt and pepper to taste

Other tasty additions are minced fresh ginger, shredded Chinese cabbage, Chinese wine and sesame oil.

You can improve the forming texture of this filling by gathering the whole mixture in your hand and slamming it into the mixing bowl with the force you would use in throwing a baseball. This breaks down the lumpiness of the ingredients so that you can make small balls that are uniform and cohesive.

Roll mixture into small balls. The mixture will yield about three dozen.

Wrapping and Frying

Pinch off pieces from your ball of dough and roll very thin. Cut in strips just wide enough to form a belt around each meat ball, leaving top and bottom open. Secure ends of the dough belt with a dab of egg white.

As you wrap them, place pork balls on a lightly oiled dish or on waxed paper well spaced so they do not touch. Otherwise, the raw dough will cause them to stick together and pull apart.

Bring peanut oil to frying temperature in your wok. A good test is to drop a small cube of stale bread into the oil. If it browns in 40 seconds, the oil is ready. Slip wrapped meat balls into the wok and deep fry 10–15 minutes. Lift out with skimmer and drain on paper toweling. Serve hot with a sauce of your own choosing.

BREAD WITH A HEART

These little yeast buns have surprises stuffed inside instead of brushed or spread on top in the Western manner. Pale they look, but there is nothing pale about their taste.

They freeze well. So it makes sense to make many at one time and solve the eternal problem of what to do with all the water chestnuts and bamboo shoots left over from other recipes. Take care to dice filling ingredients finely: it will make the difference between having a *bao* that is a treasure and one that is only coarse. And be stingy with hoisin sauce — a scant teaspoon for 2 cups of filling.

Dough
>   4½ cups unbleached flour
>   ½ cup sugar
>   1 teaspoon salt
>   1 package active yeast
>   1½ cups lukewarm water
>   1 tablespoon melted shortening

Dissolve yeast in ½ cup of the warm water. Sift flour, sugar and salt together and stir in remaining warm water and shortening. Add yeast mixture and mix well. Knead for about five minutes, let dough rest 30 minutes covered in warm place while you prepare fillings.

All fillings are made with cooked, ready-to-eat meats and provide an unusual way to use leftovers. You will need roughly two cups to fill the 24 buns you can make with this recipe.

Four Fillings

*Barbecued pork seasoned with hoisin sauce, soy, green onions and Chinese parsley

*Chinese sausage with same seasonings

*Cooked pork or ham, mushrooms, bamboo shoots, water chestnuts and the same seasonings

*Chicken, mushrooms, bamboo shoots, water chestnuts, green onions, celery and seasonings

Filling and Steaming

Pinch off plum-size pieces of dough and flatten on a breadboard. Place 1 level tablespoon filling in center. Pull dough up over filling and pinch edges together. Place pinched side down on a 2x2 inch square of waxed paper. Let rise in warm place until double in size, about 1½ hours.

Place buns in your wok on a rack above boiling water. Cover and steam for 15 minutes. Allow to cool if you plan to freeze them. Or serve hot.

Yield: 24 buns

PARTY DUMPLINGS

If you think, as we do, that Mother's dumplings are the last word in soup ornaments, you will want to add these Chinese stuffed dumplings to your kitchen repertoire. They are a special treat during Chinese New Year, but the Chinese know a good thing when they taste it and eat them the year round. They are a compliment to the unexpected guest and make good midnight snacks. They are spoon food. Select from two versions — rolled and sweet or kneaded and filled with meat.

SNOW BALLS – THE ROLLED NUT DUMPLINGS

You have probably guessed that these dumplings are rolled like snowballs. They are really a boiled cookie distantly related to baklava, but easier to make.

Prepare a mix with:
½ cup each finely chopped walnuts and almonds
½ cup ground toasted sesame seeds
12 chopped watermelon seeds (Optional. These are harder to break into than Fort Knox!)
½ cup sugar
2 tablespoons shortening
¼ cup sweet rice flour
1 egg white, beaten stiff
Enough sweet rice flour to roll balls — about 1½–2 cups

Chill mix and then form ½-inch balls. (Mix will keep several days without spoiling if stored in tightly covered glass or stainless steel bowl.)

Spread thin layer of rice flour on waxed paper.

Gently roll balls first in flour then quickly in a saucer with water barely covering the bottom. Repeat process twice more. Do not moisten balls after last rolling.

Bring 6 cups water to boil in wok. Put balls in. Cook 5 minutes after water returns to boiling. Add a cup of cold water to fix dumpling skins. Return to boiling and cook 2 or 3 more minutes.

Serve dumplings hot or cold with their "soup" thickened with corn starch, sweetened with sugar and spiked with rum or brandy, or flavored with lemon or almond extract. Allow 4 to a bowl. Two is never enough. Three is unlucky.

Yield: 8 servings

KNEADED MEAT DUMPLINGS

Dough
   1 cup sweet rice flour
   ½ cup warm water to make soft dough

Knead until smooth. Form a long roll 1 inch thick and 24 inches long.

Filling:
   Combine
   1 cup minced pork
   1 minced green onion
   2 tablespoons soy
   ½ teaspoon sugar
   ½ teaspoon sherry
   1 tablespoon cornstarch
   ½ teaspoon sesame oil

Cut dough into sections of one inch. Make a pocket with thin walls with each section and fill with a tablespoon of meat mix. Close dumplings by pinching top ends together.

Bring six cups of water to boil in your wok and put dumplings in carefully. When water returns to boiling, continue cooking until dumplings bob up.

Serve at once in bowls and eat these dripping delights with a spoon. The soup is delicious.

Yield: 24 dumplings

TEA ROOM TIMES

When I was courting my wife, I hoped to touch her heart with my knowledge of the mysterious East. I also wanted to test her spirit of adventure. After all, I was old fashioned and planned a long and, hopefully, merry life with her!

So I invited her, one day, to have "little hearts" and ducks' feet at San Francisco's famous Hangah Tea Room. "Ducks' feet are among their specialties," I informed the startled lady.

I did not learn at that time what a culture shock this was for her. Despite her innocence of how to tackle ducks' feet and her previously complete ignorance of the bird, she accepted the dish with good grace and complimented it for its succulence. She confessed this was all very new to her, no matter how old it was to the Chinese, and this confession alone endeared her to me.

I felt I was making headway in the proper fashion and promptly ordered a dish of good luck noodles to celebrate the occasion. I never hoped she would prepare ducks' feet or such noodles for me, but she has as you can see for yourself below. This is to say nothing of many other "little hearts" you will find in this book. It is her turn now to touch my heart and test my spirit of adventure.

DUCKS' FEET

This recipe is like a tune that is always played by ear: the tune is constant enough but the expression is an individual matter.

From your poultryman, buy two ducks' feet for each guest. If outer skin has not been removed, scald and remove. Wash and clean ducks' feet and remove toenails.

Heat wok with vegetable oil that has been salted and stirfry ducks' feet 3 minutes. Add some soy, rice wine (or gin), ginger slices and a little star anise.

Add 4 tablespoons water, cover and simmer until tender. Stir occasionally and add a little water if wok begins to dry out.

Isn't that easy? If you like, you can vary the dish by using bean curd or oyster sauce instead of star anise.

A BIRTHDAY DISH – FRIED NOODLES

Noodle dishes are to the Chinese what birthday cakes are to the Americans. Birthday parties always include at least one noodle dish to wish the guest of honor a long life. How nice a compliment, then, to make them fresh.

The YWCA ladies from Peking have a fresh noodle recipe that must be intended to feed an army — 8 eggs and 8 cups of flour and enough cold water to make a stiff dough. The mere thought of kneading this mountain of toughness is really too much. Instead, we suggest scaling the recipe down to small family size.

Making Fresh Noodles

2¼ cups unbleached flour
2 eggs beaten with ½ teaspoon salt
1 tablespoon salad oil
1 tablespoon water

Combine beaten eggs, salt, oil and water in a
bowl and slowly add flour to make stiff dough.
Knead for about five minutes until dough is
smooth. Roll out as thin as possible on a lightly
floured board. Cover and hold for 20 minutes.
Then roll up like a jelly roll and cut in 1/8 inch
strips. Spread out to dry for one hour.

Yield: about 4 cups

Boiling Noodles

Bring six cups water to boil in the wok. Put
dried noodles in, stir until water boils again and
cook for five minutes. Drain in colander and run
cold water over noodles. Shake water out, sprinkle with salt and stir in just enough oil to prevent
sticking and set aside.

Preparing Sauce

2½ cups shredded pork
6 fresh or 4 dried mushrooms slivered
    (remove stems)
3 green onions slivered in 1-inch sections
2 shredded bamboo shoots
2 stalks shredded celery

Set these ingredients aside in bowls while you
make ready a dish with 2 tablespoons soy and a
cup of bean sprouts. Then prepare a garnish with:

2 beaten eggs
½ cup diced ham

Into a heated, oiled wok pour one tablespoon of
beaten egg at a time and fry like a pancake.
Shred egg cakes and set aside with diced ham.

Frying Noodles

Heat wok with 3 tablespoons oil. Stir noodles, lifting them out of the wok with the turner and shaking them down. When noodles are coated with oil, turn out into a bowl and hold.

Stirfry pork, onions and mushrooms three minutes. Add celery, bamboo shoots and soy. Fry two minutes.

With clean wok fry bean sprouts in oil, add salt to taste and 1/3 cup soup stock to make a thin sauce. Return noodles and meat mixture. Heat thoroughly and serve on a platter garnished with shredded egg and ham.   Yield: 6 servings

You can vary this dish to your heart's desire with fresh shrimp, chicken, radishes, pea sprouts, fresh ginger, spinach, lettuce — anything you think tastes good at the moment. There are really no hard rules about how much of any ingredients you introduce except, perhaps, for seasonings. Put in whatever will please the guest of honor if you are making this for a birthday party.

GOURMET GIBLETS

On lazy weekends, we often bake chicken à l'Irène so named around our house for a member of the family who discovered a recipe so simple a child can accomplish it with signal success. One twist we

have added seems to stem from our Oriental bias. We toss whole giblets into the sauce that goes on the chicken during the last half hour of baking. On at least one occasion an Oriental friend has spied them in the sauce and "lifted" them as *pièces de résistance*.

The following recipes prove what delicious things happen to these tag-end items when a Chinese cook corrals them in a wok.

CHICKEN GIZZARDS HOT OR COLD

2 cups gizzards
½ teaspoon salt
2 tablespoons soy sauce
1 tablespoon rice wine
Star anise

Skin and trim gizzards. Bring 3 tablespoons vegetable oil in wok to frying heat with salt. Stirfry gizzards for 2 minutes. Add soy, wine and several points of anise. Fry briefly. Add ¼ cup water, cover and simmer until tender. Stir occasionally and add water, if necessary. Slice and serve hot or cold.

COLD CHICKEN LIVERS

You can get a head start on your party by preparing these a day ahead and storing them in the cooking liquid.

2 cups chicken livers
Thin slice fresh ginger
1 chopped green onion
1 tablespoon rice wine
3 tablespoons soy sauce
1 tablespoon sugar
Several points of star anise
Pinch of red pepper
1 cup soup stock

Wash livers. Put all ingredients together with liver. Bring soup stock to boil in wok, and put in livers. Bring to second boil and reduce heat. Cook for 15 more minutes, checking occasionally to see that wok doesn't dry out. Hold in liquid until you are ready to use. Slice and serve.

HOT CHICKEN GIZZARDS AND DUCK LIVERS

2 cups gizzards
2 cups livers
½ teaspoon salt
½ teaspoon light soy sauce
1 teaspoon rice wine
White of one egg
1 tablespoon cornstarch
½ cup vegetable oil for deep frying

Skin gizzards and cut in two. Cut livers in two. Dip in boiling water, drain. Stir in mixture of eggwhite, cornstarch, wine, and soy. Bring oil to frying temperature in wok. Fry gizzards first and then livers. Fry until brown. Serve hot. Let guests salt and pepper them to taste. We think they are perfect from the wok.

CHINESE SPARERIBS

No Chinese-style collation worth the name skips spareribs. You will want to try this easy way to culinary fame.

Trim fat and chop a side of spareribs in one-inch portions.
Make a sauce with:

> **2 tablespoons brown bean sauce**
> **1 clove minced garlic**
> **1 piece minced fresh ginger**

Stirfry sauce in 3 tablespoons oil in wok. Add spareribs and continue frying for one minute.

Add ¾ cup water and 1 tablespoon sugar and bring to boil. Reduce heat and simmer 20–25 minutes. Glaze with paste of 2 teaspoons cornstarch in 1 tablespoon cold water. Garnish spareribs with minced green onions and Chinese parsley.

CHUNGKING – FINISHING SCHOOL FOR PEANUTS

My stay in Chungking was during the humid, hot and buggy months. Mist from the Yangtze and Chialing Rivers and the perpetual haze of charcoal smoke combined to engulf us in constant murk. If we could see any kind of shadow when we held out our hands, we cleared aircraft for departures.

I worked on one side of the Yangtze and lived on the other. After each day's work, I took a 15-minute rickshaw ride from the center of the city to the bluffs overlooking San Hu Pa Airport in a sandbar in the Yangtze.

Before descending the bluffs, I cased the little clutches of merchants who sold roasted chestnuts or juicy tangerines as big as grapefruit. Usually, I settled for a tangerine or two, stuffed them in the blouse of my uniform and started clambering down scores of stone steps to the sandbar.

Still walking, I crossed the bar, making sure no planes were taking off or landing. I ploughed through deep sand to a small pier to embark on a motor launch.

This was the most dangerous part of commuting each night. There was an enormous crush of sampans, junks, boats large and small, some deep in the water and being steered downstream, others being hauled upstream along the banks by chanting coo-

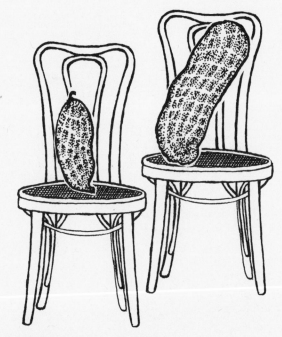

lies. Ten minutes of fighting swift currents and we were on the other side.

Another climb up the bluffs and I was home. My mosquito boots disappeared with all their dust to be cleaned for another day. I showered and went to the common room of the compound. There we played liar's dice at round tables and until dinner ate marvelous hot peanuts and drank tea.

The peanuts gave me reason to believe the old saw that whatever grows in China, grows better in Szechwan.

It is a curious fact that the peanut is an immigrant to China from the New World, its origin probably the temperate regions of Brazil and its transmitter to China an American missionary.

This "earth seed" appears on ancient specimens of Peruvian pottery. Almost every mummy of Incan and Pre-Incan people had its ration of peanuts to serve the spirit on its journey to heaven.

The peanut isn't a nut at all, but a bean and the Chinese know what to do with it. The ancient Peruvians would have loved the Chinese way.

Here are two recipes that call for blanched raw peanuts. You can buy these in a Chinese grocery store or any health food store or nut shop.

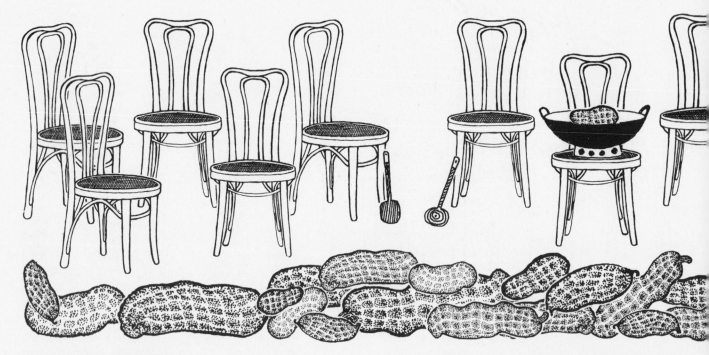

STAR ANISE PEANUTS

Bring 4 cups of water to boil in wok with ½ cup coarse salt, ½ cup sugar, 1 teaspoon rice wine vinegar and a few points of star anise. Add 3 cups raw blanched peanuts and continue boiling for two minutes. Cool nuts in liquid for five minutes, drain and spread on cookie sheet with scattering of star anise to dry over night.

Roast in moderate oven for 10 minutes, stir and reduce oven to 250° and bake another 15 minutes. When you take them from the oven, let them stand for a bit, otherwise they tend to be a bit spongy. A brief rest and they are crisp until they are all gone. If you can keep them long enough, store them in a tightly capped jar.

FIVE SPICES PEANUTS

Like the peanuts with anise, these peanuts make any you have ever had seem tasteless. The sesame oil provides a light glaze and subtle taste.

Over 2 cups of raw blanched peanuts, pour a hot mixture of ¼ cup water, 1 teaspoon salt and ¼

OTHER NUT MAGIC

Hardly content with glorifying the peanut, the Chinese have ways with freshly shelled walnuts, cashews and pecans that will drive dieters mad. Get these nuts at a health food store and prepare to test your self control.

WALNUT AND CASHEW NOUGATS

Pour one cup of boiling water over 1½ cups shelled walnuts or cashews. (If you want to do both nuts, do the cashews first when you come to the frying as they fry faster.) Let nuts stand in hot water for 2 minutes and drain. Add ½ cup cane sugar and stir lightly until nuts are completely coated. Place on cookie pan fitted with waxed paper and let stand over night.

Heat ½ cup vegetable oil in wok and bring to frying temperature. Deepfry nuts quickly a few at a time until golden. This is a very sticky operation. Sugar carmelizes on the nuts, completely coating them. Use one fork to take them from wok and a second fork to push them onto a buttered pan or tin plate. Keep them separated unless you *want* them to stick together.

Sinfully delicious. Also delicious are deepfried walnuts that are drained on paper toweling and simply dusted with powdered sugar.

teaspoon Five Spices Powder. Stir thoroughly. Spread peanuts on cookie sheet, add 3 or 4 drops of sesame oil, stir again and place in a 275° oven. Bake for an hour, stirring at 10 minute intervals. Serve warm or cold. Even a big Gay Nineties nut cup will not hold enough for each guest.

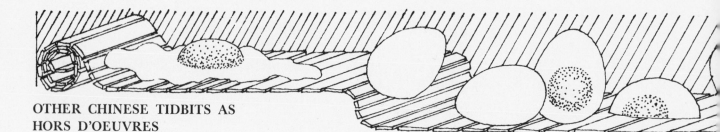

OTHER CHINESE TIDBITS AS HORS D'OEUVRES

EGGS BATIK

Like duck's feet, these are conversation pieces. The delicate traceries on the eggs are reminiscent of batiks. You start, of course, with fresh, clean eggs. If you want to experiment, you can try a limited recipe like this:

Place four large fresh eggs in 2 cups of cold water with 1 tablespoon litchi black tea and a scant tablespoon soy sauce. Bring to boil. Remove eggs and dash with cold water. Gently crack the shells without breaking them and return to the tea liquid and finish hard boiling.

Eggshells will turn a golden brown in about 7 or 8 minutes. Remove eggs from the tea and cool in the shells. Serve cold with shells removed and accompany with sweet-sour pickles. The litchi tea imparts a faintly sweet taste. You can color the eggs also with a combination of tea, salt and star anise.

EGG ROLLS

These make a satisfyingly hearty snack for your buffet.

1 cup pork
4 dried mushrooms presoaked
1 large bamboo shoot
2 tablespoons sherry
2 tablespoons light soy
7 eggs beaten with a little salt and pepper

Finely chop pork, mushrooms and bamboo. Stir-fry pork and mushrooms together in wok. When thoroughly cooked, add bamboo shoots, wine and soy. Cook about ten minutes and set aside.

Drop large spoonfuls of beaten egg — a spoon at a time — into clean, oiled wok. Tip and roll pan to make thin, even pancakes. When egg cake sets, spread with thin layer of meat filling. Using your turner, roll filled egg cake up like a crepe. Brown both sides and serve hot.

Execution of this recipe is so simple and easy that you might give a demonstration and then ask your guests to share the excitement of Wokcraft by offering them aprons and asking them to fry their own egg rolls from the ingredients you have already prepared.

While this is going on, you can make a thin sauce to spoon over the rolls, if you like. Simply dissolve a tablespoon of cornstarch in a cup of cold soup stock or the water from soaking the mushrooms, season to your taste and heat until mixture thickens and clears. Serve in a small bowl and let guests spoon the sauce over the crepes they have made.

Yield: 12–15

You can also make egg rolls with crab meat, shredded mushrooms and vegetables. Crab rolls are made larger and are served, cut in sections.

CHINESE DIP

You can make a delicately pink colored dip by mixing equal parts of pickled red bean curd, fresh bean curd and cream cheese. Add ¼ teaspoon lemon juice to each 3 tablespoons mixed dip.

Our favorite on the hors d'oeuvres tray combines crispness, freshness of color and a smooth, slightly nippy taste, reminiscent of caviar. It is a canapé made with a slice of hard boiled egg on the toast round topped with a dollop of *Chinese Dip* and garnished with minced green onion tops.

Use the dip, of course, with crackers and assorted chips.

40

CELESTIAL SOUPS

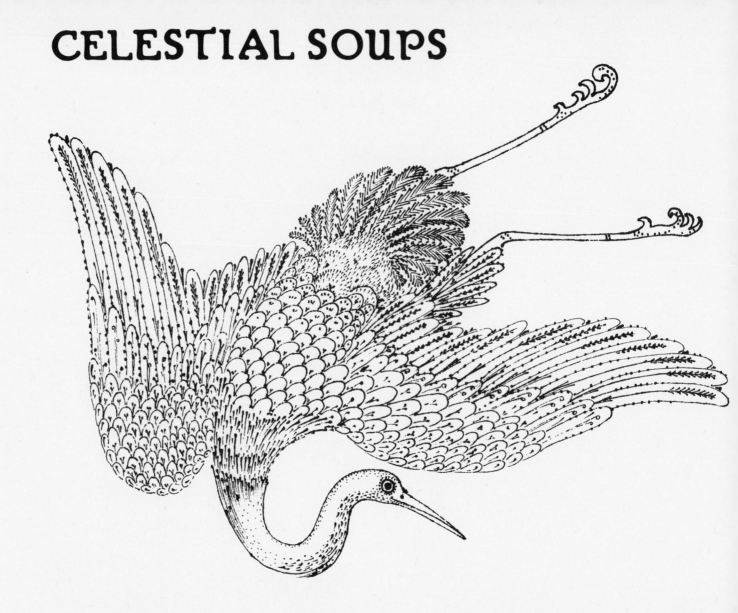

My staff in Hong Kong considered a company-sponsored banquet as important as a raise in salary. They anticipated the fun of joshing pretty waitresses, drinking hot rice wine and eating the finest food in the world in elegant surroundings. They cherished the pictures it was customary to take as a record of the happy occasions.

Such a feast celebrated my arrival in Hong Kong. Invitations were conveyed on red paper printed in Chinese and English. The affair was arranged for 7 p.m. at the Golden Dragon, an ornate pagoda-like restaurant with five floors of dining rooms. Guests entered by an open arcade paved with glistening terrazzo and arrived at their appointed diningrooms in a grill-enclosed elevator.

At street level was a page boy wearing a pillbox cap and bright green coat with brass buttons. He snapped to attention, opened the elevator door, and announced our imminent arrival by phone to the manager of the fifth floor.

From our moving cage we could see activity on each floor we passed — waiters moving in the halls but no guests — they were all hidden behind teak-wood partitions and lattice-louvered swinging doors.

At the fifth floor, the manager ushered us to our banquet room. It ran the length of the building and had windows at each end overlooking the street.

On one wall hung a huge oval mirror, etched with grasses and an egret on one side and inscribed with a poem on the other. The opposite wall was bright with a Chinese embroidery of flowers, egrets and ideographs.

A large round table was already set with ivory chopsticks on silver rests and tiny shot-size silver cups. Chairs lined the wall

Near one window was a small table with a bowl of watermelon seeds.

Almost exactly one hour after the appointed time, the host arrived fashionably late, hung his walking stick over a coat hook on the wall and we all sat down. Festivities began.

Two attractive young waitresses entered accompanied by waiters who carried heavy dishes and placed them in the center of the table. The presence of A Lung and May Choy added much to the party spirit. They were smart, spoke English well enough to get along, and they carefully noted what each of us especially liked so they could keep our plates supplied with hard-to-reach delicacies we favored.

The banquet was my first introduction to hot rice wine and *Gan-bei* — dry glass. Toast followed toast to CNAC and its future, to PAA and its five captains, and never neglect the fish! This magnificent ornament baked with its head intact, its skin basted with sauces to an unbelievable crispness, was served up with a red sweet-sour sauce. Sea bass was never like this!

No one, alas, warned me to do little more than taste each dish. When I thought the meal must be surely coming to an end, dishes kept arriving — pigeons, mushrooms, chicken with walnuts, thousand-year-old eggs, bird's nest soup, beef with vegetables. Only when I felt like a nine-year-old who had eaten too much Thanksgiving dinner did they bring in the last course — a bowl of sweet rice molded with fruit in the shape of a star. I could hardly touch it.

And more came. Now the waitresses quartered oranges and cunningly peeled back the skin from the ends so that we could hold them and eat the fruit with little effort.

The feast had reduced us to shirtsleeves by the time a photographer arrived to memorialize the event. Tea was served. The banquet was over, after four hours.

Down in the street I found the sidewalk crowded with rickshaws and bawling urchins, hawking newspapers or begging. I pushed through to a rickshaw that looked clean and in good condition. "The Gloucester," I said. The man picked up the stays, I tilted back and we swept away pursued by a child who wailed, "Tai pan, no papa, no mama, no whiskey soda!" It took six blocks to shake him.

What an evening it had been and how good China and the Chinese were to me!

This had been my first experience with the subtle flattery of Chinese banquets — the lavishness of the menu, the utter magnificence of individual dishes like the sea bass, the expense-be-damned offering of special delicacies, the extravagance of the toasts, and the obvious desire to please with the service as well as the food and the company.

The customs and symbolisms became clear only later.

Among the expense-be-damned offerings that night was the bird's nest soup which is both rare and every expensive. The main ingredient is a swallow's nest found in sea caves in the Malayan Archipelago. The edible portion of the nests is a gelatinous material that binds the twigs together and the search for the nests is fraught with dangers of slippery rocks and snakes.

Like so many things, the maiden nest is the best; the used one, less desirable; and a nest thrice used, least desirable, being thin and impure.

You buy them whole or broken by the pound. The whole ones are best.

Being able to afford them is only the first step. Now you soak the nest in cold water for several hours. Then pluck the tiny feathers and down by tweezer from the gelatinous material. This takes hours. If you persevere and reclaim the jelly, the rest is simple. Place jelly in a clear chicken stock in which there is no fat, simmer 30 minutes and

serve with a garnish of your best chopped Virginia ham.

So Chinese soups are not simply to raise your taste buds, though they do. They compliment your guest if they are of shark fins and bird's nest. They wish him a long life if they are full of noodles. There is a chicken wine soup that promises to revive the spirits and speed the recovery of new mothers.

Soups are essential to the Chinese menu whether the meal is a banquet or a modest dinner at home. It is customarily served in a tureen and ladled into the guest's bowl. Quite often it is slightly thickened with cornstarch. A banquet may begin with a creamy soup and end with a light vegetable soup. A rich soup may follow a light dish and a light soup follow a rich dish.

Simple soup stocks are the basis for many excellent Chinese soups. Clear chicken broth you can buy by the can and infuse with presoaked Chinese mushrooms and pickled cabbage. Pork stock you will have to make yourself. We add to the stock pot any liquids left over from parboiling vegetables, however small the amount, and liquids from canned vegetables, especially green beans and mushrooms. These extras always enrich sauces and soups.

A SOUP THAT STARTS IN THE WOK

PORK STOCK WITH VARIATIONS

1 cup chopped pork, minced fine and marinated in:
¼ teaspoon salt
1 teaspoon soy
1 teaspoon oil

Quickly stirfry 1 thinly sliced green onion, top and all. Add pork and continue stirfrying until it is lightly browned. Pour in 6 cups of water and simmer for ½ hour.   Yield: 6 servings

Complete pork soup with these variations:

1 package frozen peas. When peas are tender, slowly add 1 beaten egg, stirring constantly.

1 pound Chinese cabbage cut in 1-inch lengths and halved. Because we like this vegetable crisp, we cook for only 3 minutes.

Cut ½ pound winter melon into 1-inch strips, remove rind and seeds and slice thin. Bring to boil in stock and simmer until melon is translucent. Slivers of fresh basil make a tasty ornament.

Add to stock, in amounts to suit your taste, shredded smoked ham, oyster sauce, black mush-rooms, diced water chestnuts, dried shrimp and egg.

Traditionally Revered Herbs

After a recent visit to Hong Kong, Mrs. Kow Yung Ng displayed for us her treasure of herbs and spices brought home for both medicines and cookery. She presented them like crown jewels. She had gone to the source for them.

Many elegant cooks like her must depend on what they can find in Chinatown herb shops. "I am going to make a chicken soup," says a housewife, and the herb seller produces a packet with the proper herbs sufficient for one pot of soup. "I can't tell you what they are," said a friend. "They are traditional for chicken soup, that's all."

And they are expensive; so the Chinese do not lavish them on soups every day.

Mystery Unveiled

As aficionados of herb soups, we were eager to experience the Chinese version and tracked down a recipe calling for six herbs in one soup. We asked Winston Chinn of Seattle's Wa Sang Grocery on South King Street whether he sold them or not.

Glancing at our recipe, he remarked admiringly, "You can't beat this soup healthwise. It is perfect for a health addict. Unfortunately, the nearest source of herbs is Vancouver."

He made special mention of two ingredients. "Red berries everyone knows, but they are expensive, about $15 a pound. And when you get the almonds, they won't be the kind you can pick up just anywhere. These are heart shaped. If you go to Vancouver, you should be able to get packets of these herbs all ready to use. In any case, you can find someone to put up a packet with the six herbs."

He recommended an herb merchant and several days later we drove off to find the herbs in Canada.

It was as young Mr. Chinn predicted. We found four of the herbs in grocery stores already packaged for soups made with chicken, rabbit, deer or lean beef. To get all six herbs together, however, we had to go to an herb shop.

There we met a helpful Chinese gentleman who thoroughly enjoyed his role as teacher and warmed to our obvious pleasure at learning something new from him.

We watched as he made up packets from herbs he gathered by handfuls from big unmarked drawers built into the wall of his shop.

We simply showed him the list of herbs with quantities required. He courteously drew the ideographic equivalents to make it easy for us and you to buy these herbs from other Chinese herb merchants. Here they are:

2 teaspoons red berries
Gay Gee
杞子

8 slices White herb
Wai Shan
淮山角

2 tablespoons dried blanched almonds
Nom Haung
南杏

2 tablespoons lotus seeds
Lien Jee
連子

1 piece dried brown fruit (optional)
Lo Han Gwoh
元肉

2 tablespoons hundred petals
Bok Hop
北合

He offered these suggestions for their use.

CHINESE HERB SOUP

Except for "hundred petals," presoak all the herbs for ½ hour. For each packet of herbs, use 6 or 7 rice bowls of already prepared pork, chicken or beef stock. Bring to boil, add herbs and simmer for 20 minutes. Two minutes before serving, add "hundred petals", adjust seasoning and serve.

Yield: 6 servings

You will never find a soup like this on the shelves of any grocery stores. If a soup can be said to be pretty, this one is, with its red berries that turn bright red orange in the pot, its white parsnippy herb, its ivory thousand petals and its heart-shaped almonds. And if you believe folk lore about shapes of food you eat, this soup should be good for your heart! At any rate, it tastes very good and has crunch. And we have pleasant memories of the affable merchant who made up the packets.

WINTER MELON SOUP

We have Americanized this favorite. The melons grow to a size so big you can hardly get your arms around them. And they are so interesting in shape and beautiful in color — a rather dusty blue green outside and exquisite white inside — that an art school director we know should be excused the conceit of treating them like art objects. He kept one for several years, as a matter of fact, and no one knows how he managed. From time to time, he brought it out to grace an arrangement of grand enough proportions to do justice to the melon.

You can buy pieces by the pound and about one half pound will do for a modest soup, like the pork variation described on Page 44.

When you are feeling extravagant, you can do a whole melon. Cut the top off and reserve. Remove the seeds and find a pot big enough to steam the melon. That may be the hardest part of the following recipe unless you take Mr. Chinn's advice and seek out a melon that is only as big as a football.

He obligingly ran a critical eye over these instructions for filling the melon:

Pour 2 cups of chicken stock into melon along with diced ham, cubed chicken, lotus seeds, mushrooms, and salt to taste. Cap melon with its top and steam until melon meat is translucent.

"Are 2 cups of stock enough?" we asked.

"Yes," he said. "You don't use a huge melon — one as big as a football is just right. That is why 2 cups of soup is enough. Any more than that and the soup will not be as tasty as it should be. Besides, in the steaming, the flesh of the melon adds its liquids to the soup."   Yield: 6 servings

The Alien Corn

Corn, which has contributed magnificently to the Chinese soup menu, is not native to China. Like the peanut, it is an American gift to the world. And like the peanut, it was cultivated by the Incas. From them, it went step by step, mile by mile, from hand to hand for thousands of miles north. It could not survive without the help of human beings to plant it, hoe it, reap it and store its seeds.

This indispensable stewardship led Indians to surround corn with mysticism, legends and religious ceremonies. According to one tribe, a spirit woman crossed America and wherever she set foot, corn and pumpkins sprouted.

It was introduced to Europe by Columbus and popularized in China by overseas Chinese after World War II. As a food crop in the Orient, corn ranks after rice and wheat in importance today.

Interestingly enough, this ancient gift of God to man is a culinary classic: practically no one has devised ways to use it that were not already known to Indians thousands of years ago . . . except maybe the Chinese!

VELVET CORN SOUP

This is a beautiful, golden soup, flecked with pink ham and afloat with clouds of egg white which royally ornament celadon soup bowls. It makes of any meal a banquet. It is hearty, but not heavy, and is still delicious the day after you make it.

Prepare stock in your wok with a small stewing hen, 6 cups of water, 4 large presoaked Chinese mushrooms, 1 tablespoon pickled cabbage and salt to taste. Bring to boil and simmer until chicken is tender.

Remove chicken. To stock, add 2 cups cream style corn you have pureed in a blender. Boil five minutes and add:

1 cup minced cooked chicken
1 tablespoon Chinese wine
2 tablespoons chopped cooked ham
2 tablespoons finely chopped water chestnuts
Salt and pepper to taste

Boil another 3 minutes and add 1 tablespoon cornstarch dissolved in ¼ cup cold water. When this infusion clears, turn off heat and slowly add well-beaten whites of 2 eggs. Mix gently. Serve hot.   Yield: 8–10 servings

SOUR AND HOT SOUP

This cheering soup I enjoyed many times in China. It is satisfyingly substantial and has a great range in textures from soft bean curd to chewy bamboo shoots. The rich pork taste blends well with the smoky mushrooms and pleasantly crosses swords with the onion garnish. It is a soup hard to categorize. Let us just say it is very satisfying, especially on a cold day.

Bring to boil and simmer for 10 minutes:

2 cups chicken stock, salted to taste
1 tablespoon soy
4 presoaked and sliced Chinese mushrooms
½ cup pieces of bamboo shoots
1 cup pork sliced in thin strips

Add:

1 cake of bean curd cubed
¼ teaspoon white pepper
2 tablespoons white wine vinegar
2 tablespoons cornstarch dissolved in ¼ cup
    water

When soup clears, turn off heat and stir in 1

beaten egg. Add a few drops of sesame oil, garnish with finely chopped green onions and serve.   Yield: 4 servings

CHICKEN WINE SOUP

This soup traditionally recuperates the spirits and bodies of mothers after giving birth — and let's not exclude new fathers! But don't wait to have a baby to find out how good this soup can be!

Connoisseurs will appreciate the play of textures, the balance between soft cloud ears and mushrooms firm-fleshed jujubes, slender lily bud knots, chewy nuts and chicken. The taste is delicate, faintly sweet and very refreshing. Brought to table in a beautiful tureen, the soup makes a brilliant display with bright red jujubes afloat among shadowy cloud ears.

1 2½ pound pullet cut in 1½-inch pieces
2 pieces sliced ginger
15 dried Chinese mushrooms
15 dried jujubes
½ cup raw, blanched peanuts
2 cups dried cloud ears
1 cup gin or Chinese wine
2 pieces rock sugar or 2 tablespoons slab sugar

1 handful dried lily buds
Water and salt to taste

You need about two hours head start with dry ingredients. Cover mushrooms with warm water and remove stems before using. Clean cloud ears thoroughly and pinch off stems and soak in warm water. Soak lily buds, remove tough ends and tie each in a single overhand knot.

When these are ready, heat wok with very little oil and brown chicken pieces. Add ginger and continue browning. Remove ginger and add jujubes and mushrooms. Cover generously with water — two finger joints above chicken — and simmer for 15 minutes until barely tender. Add gin and continue simmering for 15 minutes. Add peanuts, cloud ears, lily buds and sugar. Simmer another 5 minutes. Salt to taste and serve from tureen. If you want to add more gin, bring heat up but *do not boil.*   Yield: 12 servings

CUCUMBER SOUP

Few things recall old friends and old times with more poignance than the memory of simple, but unfulfilled, wishes. Such a memory and an old friend come together at the thought of cucumbers — those homely gourds with the light, summer touch.

Dr. Hsien-zu Yang, a pediatrician hardly taller than her small patients and so a constant delight to children — was far from her native Changsha in the alien Middlewest when we heard her wish fervently for a cucumber soup. At the time we thought the cucumber was always "cool." How we wish we could roll back the years and offer her this soup with both hands!

1 cucumber, pared, seeded and cut in quarters
**   lengthwise, then sliced in ¼-inch pieces**
½ cup slivered ham
3 cups chicken stock
1 beaten egg
Salt to taste

Bring soup stock to boil and add ham and cucumber pieces. Cook 5 minutes. Reduce heat, drizzle in beaten egg, stirring gently. Serve hot. We add to the broth slivers of fresh herbs from

the garden. This gives the soup some sparkle against the pale green and pink of the vegetable and meat. Yield: 4 servings

FIRECRACKER OR SINGING RICE SOUP

The audio-sensation of this soup matches the visual dramas of shish kebabs on flaming swords and cherries jubilee. Elmer Wheeler who popularized "sizzle" as the key word to sell a steak probably never heard the exciting crackle of Chinese Firecracker Soup. If he had, he might have invented a Sino-sizzling term instead.

Any thin clear soup stock will do — beef, pork, chicken or seafood. The secret is to bring to table a tureen of boiling hot soup and plunge red hot browned rice crust into it before your guests' eyes. The soup sings, hisses and sizzles. No matter how often you have had this treat, you anticipate the sound and enjoy it like some great natural phenomenon.

Planning is important. Prepare the rice crusts a day or two ahead. And draw up a menu that will free you to devote the minutes just before dinner to finishing the soup and deepfrying the rice. It is wise, too, to rehearse with pots, pans, dishes and procedures so that the trip from stove to dinner table progresses smoothly.

Spread cooked glutinous rice evenly on a greased cookie sheet and bake in 250° oven. Some reputable cooks allow 5 hours for this, some 8 hours.

From time to time during the baking, turn the rice with a spatula and break into bite size chunks. When rice is done, cool and store in a tight container, or airtight bag, in the refrigerator. The rice so prepared will keep for several weeks.

To serve, deepfry rice pieces in wok until they are golden. Drain lightly and bring to table on hot tray and immediately deliver to tureen of hot soup. And stand back for the adulation of your guests!

By now you are saying, "There must be an easier way!" There is.

The Easy Way

When you make rice, you have the beginnings of rice crusts that can be used in making singing rice. Simply continue the heat *after* the rice is done, being careful not to scorch it. Dry the rice out for several hours and deepfry it just before you sizzle it into the hot soup. If crusts tend to fall apart, brush them lightly with egg yolk before deepfrying.

Variation

The singing rice technique is also effective when the sizzle is invoked by pouring a prepared thick soup or sweet-and-sour sauce entree over the rice.

The soup or entree, in this case, is prepared first and held in a warming oven while you deepfry the rice crusts as directed above. The sizzling takes place when you pour the soup or sauce over the rice at table.

JOOK, CONGEE, KANJI

This Chinese sipping dish summons memories of the eternal pot of essences that bubbled at the back of Grandmother's wood stove, picking up a bone here, leftover meats and juices there, fresh vegetables until it became a thick soup, sometimes topped with dumplings.

A San Francisco restaurant specializes in jook and every Chinese home enjoys it for breakfast and midnight snacks as well.

A basic family or party size recipe calls for:

2 cups carefully washed oval grain rice
5 quarts of water or clear broth
2 tablespoons chopped pickled cabbage
2 beaten eggs
Salt to taste

Bring liquid to a vigorous boil and add rice, 2 tablespoons at a time. Keep water boiling all the time you are adding rice; this will keep rice from sticking to bottom of pan and no stirring will be necessary. Reduce heat to medium and continue boiling rice gently, until done, about 1½ hours. During last 5 minutes of cooking add pickled cabbage and beaten eggs, stirring constantly. Adjust seasoning. You can add soy sauce to taste and garnish with chopped Chinese parsley and minced green onions. Serve boiling hot.

Made for Inventive Variations

More like a soft soup than a pudding, jook has as many variations as an imaginative cook can devise. Jooks are made with ground pork, chicken, turkey, ham bones, bits of squid, fish, duck, beef, salt-eggs, shrimp and any other colorful things you fancy.

50

A FEAST OF COLOR, TEXTURES & TASTES

Runaway inflation in the China of 1945-46 added extravagance and unreality to living in what was for me an already extraordinary environment.

Each month I received an expense advance of CN$100,000. It was enough to make me feel like a lord — on paper. In fact, simple table salt cost CN$8,000 a pound. I still have a mounted wood-cut that cost CN$80,000, though bargaining began at CN$100,000. Had I coveted a new Ford at the time, the price would have been astronomical — US$15,000! CN$1,000 was only fifty cents US, but US$15,000 was exactly US$15,000.

To avoid stuffing all my pockets with small bills, I started each month with one hundred CN$1000 bills. The day I took three friends to lunch in Shanghai, I literally dropped a bundle.

The restaurant was on Nanking Road. The occasion was sentimental. I was returning home and wanted to honor my Chinese friends who had so often honored me.

I was prepared for grand gestures. When the check came, I felt like Croesus. It was for CN$30,000. By the time I had counted out the thirty thousand-dollar bills and added CN$3,000 for a tip, I felt I had bought the restaurant. It was anticlimactic to return to my office by rickshaw for only CN$800.

The food had been superb and worth every one of the thousands of dollars. Many cultures crossed in this great river city, and there you could sample the best of both Northern and Southern styles of Chinese cooking.

THE $30,000 MENU

You have probably never expected to come into $30,000 worth of recipes from Shanghai, but here are the menu and recipes as I recall them.

Winter melon soup
Pink Shrimp with Green Peas
Chicken with Walnuts
Rice
Beef with Tomatoes and Peppers
Dragon's Eye Crème (For want of a name!)
Tea

The meal was splendidly Chinese, colorful, delicious and satisfyingly varied in textures. In a really cosmopolitan city like Shanghai, it was not surprising that there was a dessert and that it was not even Chinese in origin or character. It was doubtless a concession to foreign tastes and it was, in this case, created with a Chinese accent.

Since I am incurably Chinese in some of my habits — I always read the end of a book first and invariably leaf through newspapers and magazines backwards — you will pardon my beginning with the dessert. My wife complains about my backward habits, but she reads upside down, which makes us even!

I have tacked Crème on this dish because that is the closest I can come to the method and create a similar dessert.

The Shanghai version was made with fresh pears and peaches, peeled and cut in bite size pieces, and canned dragon's eyes. The fruit was folded into a cloud of rich, honey-sweet whipping cream laced with liqueur and sparklets of fresh orange rind. It was served in individual bowls at the end of the meal. Its reception by my guests convinced me I had acquitted my role as host with éclat.

We have made this dessert with fresh peaches and pears and seedless white grapes, marinating the fruit briefly in orange juice and slivers of orange peel while we get the whipping cream ready. When the cream is thick enough, we add a spoonful of sugar and enough Drambuie to linger on the taste. Then we drain the fruit and fold the cream about it.

But let us move on to other dishes on the menu and a whole collection of old favorites. With just one aside, perhaps: we did not run into slivers of orange — and lemon — peel in a fruit dessert again until years later. We were dining at that intimate little luncheon spot Dione Lucas had in Upper Manhattan. After a luncheon of omelets with red caviar and one with flaming rum, we ordered a fruit compote and there were the chips of orange peel spicing the dish. Whatever the dish, the addition of slivers of rind impart an incredible freshness. Try this.

Cooking with Nuts

The best nuts we ever had, we found under the Christmas Tree packed in red and green cheesecloth bags along with peppermint ribbon candy, popcornballs, oranges and apples. There were walnuts, hazelnuts, almonds, Brazil nuts and peanuts — one bag for each child in the family.

They were treats to be cracked and eaten whenever we liked. It never occurred to us that they might be eaten any other way or that we might learn new ways with nuts from the Chinese.

The Chinese, of course, eat nuts as snacks, too. They make them sinfully delicious as we have already observed. And the way they cook with almonds, cashews, chestnuts, ginkgo nuts, peanuts and walnuts is something else very wonderful.

CHICKEN WITH NUTS

This recipe is from a Hong Kong cooking school and is old enough to be your Grandmother's.

1 cup shelled walnuts
Marinate 1 boned and diced chicken in:

2 teaspoons rice wine
2 teaspoons light soy
Salt to taste
2 pieces fresh ginger, smashed
2 minced green onions
1 egg white
1 teaspoon cornstarch

Soak 2 dried mushrooms in hot water
Thinly slice 3 tablespoons bamboo shoots

Mix and hold a sauce made with:

1 teaspoon cornstarch in 3 tablespoons water
1 teaspoon sugar
2 teaspoons rice wine
Few drops of sesame oil

Let walnuts stand in boiling water for 5 minutes. Dry and deepfry in light oil in wok, being careful not to let them brown too much. In some of the same oil stirfry chicken pieces quickly until pieces turn white, add bamboo shoots and mushrooms that have been diced. Finally, add sauce, stirring until it thickens. Toss in walnuts and serve.   Yield: 6 servings

This recipe is also good with deepfried almonds, cashews and pecans as well as chestnuts. There is nothing to stop your putting more than one kind of nut in the dish or of chopping nuts finely and using them as garnish along with minced parsley to add color. Some cooks like to add a whisper of hoisin sauce at the last minute.

PORK WITH PEANUTS

Crisp, chewy, Five Spices roasted peanuts (See Page 37) lift this pork dish out of the ordinary. Carrots give it lively color. Deliciously different.

2 cups diced lean pork
2 teaspoons soy

2 teaspoons brandy
1 teaspoon cornstarch
Salt to taste
1 clove crushed garlic
1 tablespoon oil
2 teaspoons oyster sauce
1 cup sliced fresh mushrooms
1 stalk thinly sliced celery
1 large carrot sliced in triangles
½ cup roasted Five Spices peanuts
½ cup water
2 finely chopped green onions

Combine pork with soy, brandy, cornstarch and salt. Heat oil in wok with crushed garlic and stir-fry pork. When pork is ready in 3 or 4 minutes, add oyster sauce, mushrooms, celery and carrots, stir and cover. Simmer 5 minutes, stirring occasionally. Add peanuts, stir. Add water and bring to boil. The dish is ready. Garnish with finely chopped onions and serve.   Yield: 6 servings

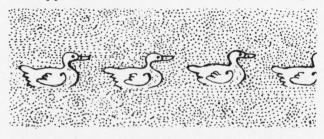

ALMOND DUCK WITH 8-PRECIOUS STUFFING

What makes this Chinese is the "precious" stuff-

ing and we come again to that charming extravagance in titling dishes so characteristic of the mystique of Chinese cuisine. Here in America we may call a dish "Supreme of Old Hen" and dream up other modestly mocking descriptions of our efforts. But the Chinese cook outreaches his imagination both when he cooks and when he tells you what he has cooked!

Because you are going to make this dish like a true believer, don't hesitate to make this stuffing even if you can't catch a 4-pound duck. A comparable chicken or turkey or a couple of Cornish hens will do as well.

First rub the bird inside and out with 2 tablespoons of rice wine mixed with ¼ teaspoon of salt. Set the bird aside for a half hour while you assemble

8-PRECIOUS STUFFING

1/3 cup ground pork
Giblets finely chopped
1 teaspoon salt
2 tablespoons rice wine
½ teaspoon mashed ginger

1 cup steamed glutinous or wild rice
½ cup chopped ham
1/3 cup shrimp chopped fine
½ cup chopped dried mushrooms, presoaked
1 green onion minced
1½ tablespoons soy
¼ cup coarsely chopped almonds
½ cup water chestnut chunks
Enough peanut oil to deepfry duck

Stirfry giblets and pork in wok. Add salt, wine, ginger and cook 2 minutes. Add remaining ingredients and mix well. Stuff and truss bird.

Place bird in a flat dish on a rack in wok, cover and steam 25 minutes to the pound. This will extract most of the duck fat and give you a bird that is succulent without being greasy. When done, remove from wok and pat dry with paper toweling.

Prepare a batter with 1 beaten egg and one complete eggshell each of unbleached flour and water. Using a pastry brush, coat bird with batter. Deepfry in wok until golden brown.

Present duck on bed of lettuce with small clusters of grapes and wedges of fresh oranges. Carve and serve.   Yield: 6 servings

You will give your guests a pleasant surprise if you borrow an old Cantonese trick in preparing the orange wedges. Cut into each end of the wedges between rind and meat so that guests can pull the peels back to eat oranges easily. I first observed this at banquets in Cantonese restaurants. Waitresses offered orange wedges, so cut, between thumb and second finger so that guests could bite off the meat and not have to handle the sticky fruit. This graceful amenity impressed me as the ultimate in service.

FRIED MILK

Almonds are an important garnish on this super-elegant and unusual dish for a Sunday brunch with fruit salad, perhaps, and muffins and toast made with home baked bread. The fluffy egg whites have a deliciously softer texture than whole scrambled eggs. The minced ham bestows both its savory taste and its pinkness to the cloud whiteness of the eggs. The satisfying crunch of the nuts brings you down to earth. As for the leftover egg yolks — plan ahead. They can go into batters of all kinds in breads, pancakes, cakes and muffins.

10 egg whites beaten until they peak
1 teaspoon cornstarch
1 teaspoon salt
1 cup of milk
¼ cup slivered almonds
1 cup finely diced cooked ham

Gradually add cornstarch and salt to milk. Fold in beaten egg whites.

Quickly deepfry slivered almonds in wok, being careful not to overbrown. Set aside. Stirfry ham in a little of the same oil and hold on a warm dish. Now fry the milk mixture in the wok, stirring constantly. When it thickens it is ready to serve at once. Garnish with ham and almonds and stand back for compliments and a toast to the cook.
If you want to serve this as a luncheon dish, place the fried eggs in a nest of hot noodles.

Fish and Sea Food

The Chinese have been fish farmers from way back. Chinese restaurants often keep fish alive and swimming until they go into the recipe.

For those who especially like sea foods and fish, the Chinese cuisine has a special attraction. It tests the cook's ingenuity to produce tastes and textures and magnificent sauces. Some of the most colorfully beautiful Chinese dishes you will make are made with them.

GREEN JADE AND RED CORAL

The name tells you that the dish will be a sight to behold.

1 pound of broccoli or any green vegetable, chopped into cubes
½ pound cooked crab meat
1 slice ginger
1 teaspoon salt
1 teaspoon sugar
3 teaspoons Chinese wine
4 teaspoons light soy
Enough vegetable oil for stirfrying

Heat oil in wok and stirfry ginger. Remove ginger and stirfry cubed vegetables together with salt, sugar, wine and soy, at least 5 minutes. Add crab and continue stirfrying 3 minutes. Serve hot.
Yield: 6 servings

PINK SHRIMP AND GREEN PEAS

This recipe is from the $30,000 luncheon. The dish impressed me especially because I had never enjoyed peas so much — so pristinely green and glistening from the wok, so happily contrasted with small pink shrimp.

1½ pounds of small shelled shrimp

2 tablespoons cornstarch
1 slice of ginger the size of a half dollar minced
2 tablespoons sherry
1 tablespoon light soy
1 cup salad oil
2 cups shelled small peas

Wash and drain shrimp and marinate for 20 minutes in the mixed cornstarch, ginger, wine and soy.

This quick cooking dish requires a substantial amount of oil in order to cook in a few minutes.

Heat oil in wok. Quickly fry peas. Remove and immediately add shrimps to hot oil with slotted spoon. The minute the shrimps turn pink, lift out with skimmer to plate. Add peas and serve with rice. Yield: 6 servings

LOBSTER CANTONESE

This lobster dish demonstrates the affinity pork has for a rich shellfish. To simplify things, we use frozen lobster tails. To fully enjoy it, plan to serve it with a very crisp green salad, plain rice and a piquant fruit compote with slivers of orange and lemon peel, for dessert.

1 cup ground pork
1 tablespoon minced bamboo shoots
1 tablespoon minced water chestnuts
1 finely chopped green onion, top and all
2 lobster tails defrosted and cut into ½-inch cubes
1 clove garlic
Salt and pepper to taste
Light oil for the wok

1 cup chicken stock
2 tablespoons rice wine
1 teaspoon sugar
2 beaten eggs

1 tablespoon cornstarch
1 tablespoon soy
¼ cup water

Mix pork, bamboo shoots, water chestnuts and onion. Add lobster cubes.

Heat wok with oil and fry garlic clove with salt and pepper. Remove garlic and add meat-fish mix. Pour in liquids and add sugar. Bring to boil and reduce heat. Cover wok and simmer for 10 minutes. Stir in eggs and continue cooking for 2 minutes.

Add water in which you have mixed the cornstarch and soy and let sauce thicken. Serve hot.

Since this is at best a pale dish, bring it to table on a colorful dish with a garnish of watercress or Chinese parsley. Besides, these tangy greens will compliment the richness of the lobster and pork.

Yield: 6 servings

DEEPFRIED, SWEET AND SOUR FISH

At every feast I ever attended, at least one toast was to the fish — the most magnificent of all the dishes. The whole fish arrived, deepfried, its head and tail intact and raised off the platter as though it were alive enough to jump and its sides deeply scored to ease serving. Over all was a splendid and colorful sauce.

My Chinese hosts offered me the choicest part from the fish cheek and more than once teased me by offering a fish eye.

A feature of the dish is an exquisite crispness of the double-fried skin. It will help to have two woks handy.

1 whole, 2-pound fish
1 tablespoon rice wine
1 tablespoon light soy
1 teaspoon lemon juice
Salt and pepper

Clean and scale fish. Slash diagonally at 1-inch intervals on each side. Rub fish inside and out with seasoning mixture of wine, soy, lemon and salt and pepper. Set aside for 20–30 minutes.

Blot fish dry after this preseasoning and roll lightly in cornstarch. Heat enough light oil in wok to deepfry fish. Place fish in a sieve and lower into hot fat. Baste often. This takes only a few minutes. When ready, remove fish, drain and hold in a warm oven until you are ready to refry.

Make sauce with:

1 cup cider vinegar
1 cup brown sugar
2 tablespoons cornstarch

In a clean wok, quickly stirfry

1 teaspoon finely minced ginger
1 minced green onion
½ cup green pepper chunks
½ cup tomato chunks

Add sauce and bring to boil.

In the first wok, refry fish in deep fat. Arrange on appropriate platter and cover with the beautiful sauce.   Yield: 4 servings

Chicken Thoughts

Let no one be so crass as to think "chicken thoughts" are craven. To us, they recall a farm on the Ottertail River long before chicken became commonplace in its instant parts display in supermarkets. No, there was that wild drama of racing around the farmyard after one of our aunts in hot pursuit of a young rooster. Magnificent squawks and finally the denouement for the bird and the beginning of preparations for Sunday Dinner.

Chicken was not common. It was special enough to be in the title of a book and potent enough an image-maker to be part of a political slogan — A Chicken in Every Pot and Two Cars in Every Garage!

Chicken was something your loving country grandmother fried to a luscious brown and packed in a little box for you to take on the train when you went back to the city after summer was gone.

With this little prelude, we bid fair to introducing the Chinese Chicken which is very special, too.

EMPRESS CHICKEN

1 cup chicken breast, boned and cut in cubes

2 spring onions cut in 1-inch lengths and halved
2 slices fresh ginger
2 tablespoons wine
3 tablespoons light soy sauce
½ cup bamboo shoots sliced matchstick size
½ cup finely sliced celery
½ cup mushroom pieces
1 tablespoon sugar

Heat about 3 tablespoons of light oil in wok. Stirfry onions, ginger and chicken. When chicken turns white, remove ginger slices and add the wine and soy and continue cooking over high heat for 5 minutes, turning chicken occasionally. Add ½ cup water or soup stock (If you are using canned mushrooms, you can add that to the stock.) and bring to boil. Reduce heat and cook covered about 10 minutes.

Add bamboo shoots, celery, mushrooms and sugar. Continue cooking until chicken is tender. At last minute add 2 tablespoons green peas. Serve piping hot.

We have used jicama with this dish with refreshing results. The texture is that of the bamboo shoots and the taste, delicately sweet, is satisfying.   Yield: 4 servings

CHICKEN BREASTS WITH SESAME

This delicate dish is one of our favorites. Cool and ambrosial on a hot summer day, it can be a make-a-day-ahead treat to be served on a bed of lettuce for a buffet. It is equally tasty hot or cold, as a salad or an entree and you can hardly find dishes like that any more! Rejoice if there are leftovers.

2 cups diced boned chicken breast
¼ cup chopped green pepper
4 tablespoons oil
2 tablespoons soup stock
2 tablespoons sugar
¼ cup Chinese plum sauce
1 tablespoon malt vinegar + 3 tablespoons pineapple juice
½ cup pineapple chunks drained
2 tablespoons toasted sesame seeds
4 thinly sliced pickled scallions
Chinese parsley for garnish

Heat oil in wok and stirfry chicken and green pepper. When chicken turns white, add soup stock, cover and cook until water cooks away. Add sauce you have prepared from remaining ingredients. When it is hot, turn out on serving dish, garnish with parsley and serve at once.

Yield: 6 servings

If we are planning a number of dishes and want to save time, we steam the chicken breasts in the wok, cool and bone, break into chunks and hold in the refrigerator with the sauce stirred in. And depending on how much color we want to introduce, we sometimes substitute mandarin oranges for pineapple.

CHICKEN WITH ZUCCHINI

This dish marries crunchiness of texture, fresh color and the homely taste of chicken and zucchini. The vegetable could just as well be asparagus in spring or celery.

1 cup diced chicken breast
1 clove crushed garlic
2 tablespoons light soy sauce

½ cup bamboo shoots sliced matchstick size
¼ cup canned mushroom slices
1½ cups diced zucchini

1 tablespoon cornstarch in ¼ cup water
Roasted slivered almonds

Stirfry chicken over high heat with garlic in oil. When it turns white, add 2 tablespoons soy, and continue stirring for several minutes.

Add zucchini, mushrooms and bamboo shoots, cover and cook a few minutes.

Add cornstarch paste and stir for about 1 minute. Garnish with roasted slivered almonds.

Yield: 4 servings

PORK STIRFRIES

PORK WITH GREEN BEANS

This is a succulent, tasty dish. The green beans are the crunchiest ingredient and their fresh green flavor permeates.

1 cup lean pork cut in thin strips
1 clove garlic crushed
1 teaspoon salt
2 tablespoons oil

2 dried Chinese mushrooms (presoaked 2 hours and sliced)
1½ teaspoons soy
1 teaspoon rice wine
¼ teaspoon sugar
½ cup bamboo shoots sliced in 2-inch lengths, shoestring width
1 stalk thinly sliced celery
½ minced green onion

¾ cup soup stock or water
1 cup green beans (parboiled 2 minutes and cut in 1-inch lengths)

2 teaspoons cornstarch
1 teaspoon sherry
1 tablespoon water
1 tablespoon oyster sauce

Stirfry garlic in oil with salt. When garlic browns, remove and add pork strips. Stirfry until meat whitens. Add mushrooms, soy, wine, and sugar mixture and continue stirfrying for several minutes.

Add bamboo shoots, celery, onion and green beans with soup stock. Bring to boil, reduce heat, cover wok and cook one minute. Stir in cornstarch mixture with sherry, water and oyster sauce. When this thickens, dish is ready.

Yield: 6 servings

SWEET AND SOUR SPARERIBS

This recipe is equally good for spareribs and bite size lean pork. Meat is deepfried.

An important ingredient is another American food gift to the world — the pineapple. Probably as ancient as the potato, it took immeasurable time for the lowlands Indians of Central and South America to develop it into the luscious, tender-fleshed fruit it is today. Vast numbers, of course, are grown in the Orient.

It is pleasant to recall that Indians used them at entrances to their villages as symbols of friendship and hospitality. British colonists followed suit and carved or painted pineapples above and beside entrances to assure strangers they would receive a friendly welcome.

Prepare a marinade with:

½ cup sugar
1 teaspoon salt
1 tablespoon soy sauce
1 beaten egg

Add to this 2 cups of lean cubed pork or 4 cups of spareribs, trimmed of fat and cut in 1-inch pieces. Allow to stand until seasonings are absorbed.

1 small green pepper cut in chunks
1 chopped tomato
1 clove finely chopped garlic
4 slices ginger chopped fine
1 yellow onion cut in chunks

½ cup vinegar
½ cup brown sugar
1 teaspoon salt
2 tablespoons cornstarch
½ cup canned pineapple chunks drained

Roll marinated pork in cornstarch, allowing cornstarch to become completely moist. Bring enough peanut oil to frying heat in wok to deep-fry pork pieces until light brown — 6 to 8 minutes. Remove from wok with skimmer and drain on paper toweling. Put aside and keep warm. Our Chinese friends, incidentally, say the secret of super spareribs is to deepfry the meat more than once.

With a clean wok, heat 2 tablespoons oil to stir-fry peppers, onion, garlic and ginger for 1–2 minutes. Add tomato chunks and sauce made with vinegar, sugar, salt, pineapple and corn-starch. When mixture thickens and clears, add pork, stir quickly and serve piping hot.

Yield: 8 servings

Beef and Bach

Beef, of course, is not the only meat conducive to so many variations. Its universal appeal, however, makes it logical to tell you that combinations you can stirfry with beef make it a basis for kitchen fugues worthy of Johann Sebastian Bach.

Snow peas, bean sprouts, asparagus, celery, carrots, Brussels sprouts, lotus root, string beans, cauliflower, zucchini, lettuce, peas — all are possible variations on the theme we have selected:

BEEF WITH BROCCOLI

You can use the broccoli flower heads as well as

the stalks for this recipe. You may notice for the first time ever what a beautiful handsome form the broccoli stalk takes when it is sliced for stirfrying — rather like those elegant and symmetrical shapes you see in the designs of Japanese family crests. So you have two treats in store: one visual and the other palatable! No wonder this dish has been included in wedding feasts along with shark's fin soup, deep fried squab, roast suckling pig, and sweet rice chicken!

1 cup lean, tender beef sliced in narrow strips
1 tablespoon cornstarch
1 tablespoon light soy

2 tablespoons oil
¼ teaspoon salt
1 finely chopped clove of garlic

2 cups broccoli stalks thinly sliced across grain
2 oz. can mushroom pieces
½ teaspoon salt
1/3 cup soup stock

Toss beef in cornstarch and soy mixture.

Stirfry salt and garlic in oil and add beef. The cornstarch, soy and beef juices will form a thin coating on bottom of wok. This dissolves when you add soup stock and forms the familiar glaze which is usually added at the last minute.

Stirfry beef to degree of doneness you prefer

and remove. In the same wok bring broccoli and mushrooms to boil with salt and stock. Cover wok, reduce heat and cook for about 4 minutes. Return beef to wok and cook briefly with cover removed. Serve at once.

Yield: 6 servings

When you are using vegetables other than broccoli for beef stirfries, keep in mind that green beans and cauliflower should be parboiled and that the more fragile green stuffs come to the right doneness quite fast. Just rely on your commonsense.

And if you like your stirfries saucier, you can add a full glaze at the last minute with:

1 tablespoon cornstarch in
1 tablespoon cold water

or

1 teaspoon soy sauce
1 tablespoon sherry
½ teaspoon sugar
A drop or two of sesame oil
1 slice minced ginger

You can also garnish the dishes with Chinese parsley, minced spring onions, minced fresh basil, or whatever the spirit moves you to do.

A Pair of Lambs

Lamb has been a rarity on the Chinese restaurant

menus we have seen in the past. But it has always been a favorite since we enjoyed Mrs. Porter's New England dinners with leg of lamb and little browned potatoes ringing the platter. The dear lady thought we cooked like foreigners but loved us all the same. She would surely have liked this stirfry lamb and especially the Ming Dynasty dish.

LAMB STIRFRY

1 cup lamb cut in thin bite size pieces

1 tablespoon soy
1 tablespoon sherry
½ teaspoon salt

2 tablespoons oil

3 spring onions quartered lengthwise and cut
   in 1-inch sections
¼ cup bamboo shoots cut matchstick size

Marinate lamb in soy, sherry and salt. Heat oil in wok and brown onions. Add lamb and bamboo shoots and stirfry 2–4 minutes. Serve at once. This dish goes very fast. Nice with rice, or try it with Armenian boulgour for a change.

Yield: 4 servings

MING DYNASTY LAMB

This spiced dish probably proves that the Ming Dynasty was famous for more than its porcelains, for we have it on the authority of the ladies from Peking that this is an authentic Ming Dynasty recipe. Exotic and pungent in aroma, the dish is too austere to be served without its gravy.

2 pounds of lamb trimmed of fat
2 teaspoons turmeric
2 teaspoons soy bean paste
1 teaspoon Five Spices

Place spices in a bag and simmer with meat for 2 hours in a tightly covered wok. Remove spices and carve lamb in thin slices. Let stand over night in liquid. Before serving, reheat meat and thicken liquid with cornstarch to make a gravy. Adjust seasoning. Serve lamb hot with gravy spooned over it. A tasty companion for lamb: cooked dried apricots.
   Yield: 6 servings

Two Dishes to Stick to Your Ribs

If you can walk away from a Chinese meal that includes fried rice or fried noodles and complain a half hour later that you are hungry, you would have to be Paul Bunyan. These dishes are easy to make, lend themselves to almost endless variations, and are vastly satisfying to the hungry.

FRIED RICE

2 cups boiled rice

1 tablespoon peanut oil
¾ cup Chinese sausage cut in thin rounds

1 tablespoon soy sauce
2 eggs beaten
2 tablespoons finely chopped green onions
1 cup lettuce chopped to slivers
   (Romaine, head lettuce, red lettuce)

Heat oil in wok and stirfry sausage pieces till fat melts. Add rice and continue stirfrying until rice is thoroughly heated and the oil evenly distributed. Add soy, mix well, add beaten eggs and stir until blended. Add lettuce and stirfry another minute. Serve garnished with chopped onion.

The eggs, incidentally, can be fried like little pancakes and cut in shreds for a garnish instead of stirring them into the rice.   Yield: 6 servings

Variations and substitutions

Instead of sausage: 1 cup diced cooked roast pork, ham, chicken or turkey; 1 cup cooked shrimp or tuna, flaked crab, lobster pieces. Note: Since Chinese sausage combines pork and pork fat with sugar, grain alcohol and soy, add ½ teaspoon sugar and 1 teaspoon Chinese wine or sherry to soy sauce when using other ingredients than the sausage.

Instead of lettuce: 1 cup bean sprouts, chopped celery, sliced water chestnuts, green peas (parboiled) bamboo shoots, diced cucumber, mushrooms (canned or fresh), finely diced green peppers, fresh stringbeans (parboiled).

Sauce substitute: oyster sauce

Garnishes: roasted chopped peanuts, almonds or walnuts.

This is a colorful dish with the yellow of egg, green of lettuce, red of sausage and white of rice. And it's ready to eat four minutes after you start cooking. Serve it with crab/cucumber relish if you like to balance the slight oiliness of the rice with a homely sour taste.

FRIED NOODLES

You can start from scratch and make your own fresh noodles. Let's assume you have. (See Page 31 Little Hearts) This is the next thing to do:

4 cups of Chinese egg noodles cooked and drained in a sieve after a dousing of cold water

2 tablespoons oil
1 cup cooked chicken cut in ½-inch chunks or shredded
1 teaspoon rice wine
½ teaspoon cornstarch
1 spring onion sliced in half and then cut in 1-inch sections

2 oz. can of mushroom pieces
1 cup ham, sliced matchstick size

½ cup bamboo shoots or water chestnuts
  chopped
½ cup green peas
1 tablespoon soy sauce
1 tablespoon sherry
½ teaspoon salt
2 tablespoons cornstarch

Marinate chicken in 1 teaspoon wine and ½
teaspoon cornstarch.

Heat oil in wok. Stirfry noodles that have become dry but not stiff. Keep turning noodles until they are completely coated with oil. Remove from wok.

Stirfry marinated chicken, ham, and vegetables for 3 or 4 minutes. Add noodles and sauce of soy, sherry, salt and cornstarch. Stirfry 2 minutes more and serve at once.

LETTUCEBURGERS, CHINESE

SALADS & EXOTIC GREENS

JOIE DE VIVRE

The Chinese are naturally and joyously convivial. Their familial feasts, their wholehearted capacity for sharing, and their wildly fun cook-ins under even difficult conditions have endeared them to us.

We once joined a Chinese potter in his little house — before he built his big house — for a feast. The oven of his vintage stove was not big enough for all the things he asked it to hold.

"By the time he stuffs it with all those pots," we thought nervously, "we'll have to tie the door closed on the oven."

Somehow he stuffed the oven . . . his long experience stacking kilns must have reinforced him . . . and the situation deteriorated into incredulous laughter.

A-LITTLE-OF-THIS-AND-A-HANDFUL-OF-THAT COOK

The hot dishes came out of the oven precariously in another hour. They brought extravagant compliments for their freight of magnificent food. We ended by congratulating ourselves that we had a wily friend who did the impossible quite simply. He believed in his stove.

Unfortunately, but typically, not a single recipe was traded that day. What went on in the kitchen, in the oven and atop the stove was all improvised. Like an impresario, our friend had produced a culinary drama — one performance only for one happy occasion.

This freewheeling cuisine is characteristic.

The Chinese have developed vegetarian cookery to a legendary art. Nina Froud recalls one of the delights of her childhood was to dine on a roast goose made entirely of soy bean curd. The occasion was a feast of 30 dishes in a Buddhist monastery — all vegetarian and many shaped as fish or fowl. The goose not only had the shape, but also the taste of real goose.

We have no such miracles for you to perform. We can only show you that the Chinese have a special gift for making the most of anything cookable.

Lettuce, for example, is more useful to them than simply as salad ingredients and garnishes. The Chinese drop it in soup to make a delicately beautiful and refreshingly crisp prelude to dinner. They shred lettuce hearts to serve as substitutes for bean sprouts in fried rice. They make it perform as an edible napkin — and thereby hangs a tale.

LETTUCEBURGERS

A gifted Chinese painter was the first who offered to prove to us that salad greens play an offbeat role in the Chinese menu. We eagerly offered the kitchen of the little house for a demonstration and invited friends to share the event.

The son of a Chinese Admiral — you must believe this — the young painter would have enjoyed the help of at least nine servants at home in China. But he made do with several young lady guests as assistants and directed them with authority. The ingredients all came from bulging big brown paper sacks.

In a manner we came to appreciate as very Oriental, he brought the affair off in the grand manner. He did not come just to prove that the Chinese do eat lots of salad greens. He came to show how magnificently balanced a whole Cantonese-style dinner can be. The demonstration absorbed us for two hours. We will remember it all our lives.

The Menu

This was the menu:

> Melon soup
> Cantonese Lettuceburgers
> Fried rice
> Chinese barbecued chicken
> Relishes of chopped pickled ginger
>   root and sweet-sour pickled scal-
>   lions sliced lengthwise

The barbecued chicken he brought from Chinatown, "because," he said, "we are not going to have time enough to do it right."

CANTONESE LETTUCEBURGERS

This is a very democratic dish and so delicious that even your stuffiest guest will love getting his fingers into it. It requires three young ladies to do the chopping, naturally!

Slice several bamboo shoots as narrow as shoestrings and set aside. Next slice very thinly one large pork chop and marinate in 1 tablespoon soy with a gift of wine and 1 teaspoon sugar.

Slice thinly, lengthwise, ½ pound sugar peas.

Heat oil in wok and quickly fry peas. Add meat mixture and fry till brown, adding soy if desired. Add bamboo shoots and cook until soft, about 3 minutes. Turn into bowl to serve.

In the meantime, you will have washed and thoroughly drained large leaves of fresh lettuce (iceberg, red or romaine). Chill and serve in separate bowl. Invite guests to serve themselves a lettuce leaf and spoon the meat mixture into lettuce leaf along with some fried rice. Then simply fold the leaf like a crepe and eat with your fingers.   Yield: 6–8 servings

Equally delicious fillings for lettuceburgers can be made from such combinations as:
Chopped, boned squab stirfried in wok with bamboo shoots, water chestnuts, ginger and a dash of brandy;
Sliced mushrooms and chopped celery stirfried;
Lean pork stirfried with garlic, peas, soy, rice wine and sugar thickened with cornstarch and garnished with fried, finely chopped almonds.

FRIED LETTUCE DELUXE

Since you have already tried this dish, reduced to its simplest form, try this more elaborate version and serve with a substantial rice dish.

1 head crisp, fresh lettuce
1 clove garlic
1 piece hot red pepper
2 tablespoons soy
Salt to taste

Chop lettuce in large pieces about 1 x 3 inches. Heat oil in wok and brown garlic with pepper, salt and soy. Remove browned garlic and add lettuce. Stirfry 1 minute.

Pour over lettuce a sauce of:

2 tablespoons water
1½ tablespoons sherry
1 teaspoon sugar
3 slivered spring onions

Toss briefly and finally glaze lettuce with a paste of cornstarch and water. When lettuce is coated, serve at once.   Yield: 6 servings

You can prepare the same dish with Chinese cabbage. Frying time is slightly longer. And don't overlook possibilities of frying spinach, radish tops, watercress, cauliflower and Brussels sprouts.

CHINESE BUNDLINGS

This recipe exploits synergism at the stove. Like Russian golubtsy and Greek dolmathakia, these Chinese cabbage rolls serve up meat in vegetable wraps, but in much less time. The recipe asks an ordinarily plain vegetable to enhance something else. The dish can be made also with Chinese sausages, beef, and lamb.

The Russian beef in cabbage and Greek lamb in grape leaves, incidentally, are prepared as casseroles and are worth your study for their contribution of such ingredients as sour cream, rice, pine nuts, spices and herbs.

Now for the *Bundlings*. They can be boiled or steamed, and they are good as leftovers.

Plunge a Chinese cabbage into boiling water and remove almost immediately. Peel off leaves and trim to uniform size — 4 x 2 inches. Save leftovers for soups.

Put 1 heaping tablespoon of the following filling on each leaf, roll up and fasten with a toothpick.

Mix: 1 pound ground pork or beef
     ½ cup chopped water chestnuts
     1 beaten egg
     1 stalk minced celery
     2 minced green onions
     2 teaspoons cornstarch
     1 tablespoon rice wine or brandy
     1 teaspoon salt

Boiled Version: Heat oil in wok and roll cabbage bundles in oil. Pour 1 cup soup stock, 1 cup mushrooms, ¼ cup chopped cooked ham over cabbage bundles and boil 5 minutes. Glaze bundles with 1 tablespoon cornstarch in 2 tablespoons water. Serve hot, garnished with Chinese parsley.

Steamed Version: Place cabbage bundles on shallow dish in wok, cover and steam for 40 minutes. Recover juice from steaming dish and add 2 tablespoons cornstarch and 1 tablespoon cold water, to thicken. Pour over bundles and serve hot garnished with Chinese parsley.

Yield: 21–24 rolls

CHINESE TRIPLE TREAT

This three-layer meal-in-a-dish lays an egg in the best sense of the word. It is hearty enough to serve to hungry teenagers. Accompany with a lettuce soup or fried lettuce and fresh fruits for dessert, if anyone is still hungry.

Mix: 1 pound ground beef
     2 minced bamboo shoots
     1 tablespoon preserved parsnips
     1 teaspoon cornstarch
     10 water chestnuts chopped
     6 fresh mushrooms chopped
     1 piece minced ginger
     ½ teaspoon brandy
     1 teaspoon sugar
     1 teaspoon soy and a few drops of
       sesame oil

Put meat mix aside while you steam 2 cups of rice 25–30 minutes. When rice is ready, spread meat mix over rice and continue steaming a few minutes. Now, carefully break one egg for each guest over meat and continue steaming until whites of eggs set. Serve at once, garnished with minced green onions and parsley.

This dish may take a little practice and depend on your taste and requirements for doneness of meat and eggs. Yield: 6–8 servings

Cucumbers and Radishes for Country Freshness

As children, we watched cucumbers grow big on the vines in a country garden and end in a bath of cider vinegar, sugar, salt and pepper. That childhood memory of cool cucumbers, harvested in a sunwarmed patch and chilled in a well, is equalled now by the Chinese way with this member of the gourd family. The sesame oil is the secret of its indescribable difference.

COOL CUCUMBERS

Pare and thinly slice 1 large cucumber. We place the rounds in a bowl and lightly salt alternate layers.

Toss in a dressing of:

3 tablespoons rice wine vinegar
1 tablespoon sugar
¼ teaspoon soy

A few drops of sesame oil

Chill and serve.

You can also use a boiled dressing made with 3 tablespoons rice wine vinegar, 2 tablespoons sugar and a teaspoon of ginger juice. Cool it and toss cucumbers. Chill before serving.

Yield: 4–6 servings

RADISHES – A CELEBRATION IN RED, WHITE AND GREEN

Prepare these at the last minute to protect the pristine sharpness of the colors, for this dish is a joy to behold.

Thinly slice a bunch of radishes and bruise them with the side of your chopper blade. You can use the same recipe for dressing as for the cucumbers, adding a crushed clove of garlic. Serve on a leaf of lettuce and garnish with chopped green onions or chives. Just a little of this piquant dish goes a long way in lifting a meal.

Yield: 6 servings

Seagoing Cucumbers

Until we ate Oriental, we never met the cucumber dish that goes to sea. At least it comes to the table with crab or shrimp. Your first encounter with it may find you concentrating on it to the exclusion of other tasty foods set before you.

CUCUMBER WITH CRAB

1 large cucumber
½ cup crabmeat broken into pieces

Dressing:
3 tablespoons rice wine vinegar
1 tablespoon soy
1 tablespoon sugar
½ teaspoon salt
A few drops sesame oil

Peel cucumber with potato parer and slice rounds very thin. Salt and chill for 20 minutes. Squeeze out liquid with your hands and sprinkle cucumbers with a little vinegar. Squeeze liquid out again.

Toss cucumbers and crab with dressing. Serve in small dishes — one for each guest — and garnish with tiny shreds of fresh ginger.

Yield: 6 servings

CUCUMBER WITH SHRIMP

The delicate color harmony of this pale pink and pale green dish recalls misty French Impressionist paintings but has the super-advantage of being edible. Use cooked shrimp.

When you prepare cucumbers and shrimp, cut the cucumber in thin, 2-inch strips and use about

12 large shrimps each chopped in about four pieces. And gently press the liquid from the salted strips as in the recipe instructions for *Cucumber with Crab*. Use the same dressing.

Yield: 6 servings

Back to the Wok for This Salad!

You may have had German Potato Salad served

hot from a skillet, but have you ever considered hot chicken salad? Made in a wok and subtly seasoned with Chinese spices?

WOK CHICKEN SALAD

Marinate two boned chicken breasts for 1 hour in:

¼ cup soy

1 grated clove of garlic
1 small piece minced ginger
4 teaspoons sugar
¼ teaspoon Five Spices Powder

Deep fry chicken in wok until golden brown.
Drain and cool. Shred and season with celery
salt and Five Spices Powder. Put in bowl and
add:

¼ cup thinly sliced green onions
½ cup thinly sliced celery
¼ cup Chinese parsley
1 head of shredded iceberg lettuce

Sprinkle with 2 teaspoons toasted sesame seeds
and a little sesame seed oil. Season with salt and
pepper to taste. Serve chilled or hot.

Yield: 6 servings

IMPERIAL FARE - PEKING DUCK

No city in the world is like Peking. No other made me feel so regal, so grand and so serene.

No other city guards and hides its secrets within medieval ramparts of such enormous size. Or places so many ceremonial stone arches across such broad avenues.

Everywhere is an unprecedented stamp of antiquity and mystery. The number and exaggerated scale of the red walls you pass through are a constant revelation of architectural elegance. I passed under the gate of one wall that was topped with a three-story dragon roofed watch tower and barracks for guards. An immense archway tunneled through 65 feet of stone. Huge doors studded with beautiful iron ornaments stood open. The visual impact was breathtaking. Passing through was literally an environmental massage.

As I approached the wall, it seemed to shrink in size while the archway grew big. Then I was inside and the wall became a collossal canopy, impressively secure. Every step I took changed the perspective. I passed from light to soft shadows into cool gloom and back to hot sunlight.

Every wall I passed through made me singularly conscious of the mounting excitement of moving through the city. Each gateway seemed more magnificent than the last. The balance of space and mass, of open courts and palace buildings was exquisite.

What names the gates had! Gate of Prolonged Righteousness, Gate of Scenery and Happiness, Gate of Heavenly Peace!

There I was inside the purple city, the world

famed Forbidden City, the Imperial residence
with 5,000 years of history in it.

It was my great good fortune to dine on Peking
Duck in a Peking restaurant famous for the dish.

My host was a gentleman whose name translated
signified "prince," and he lived up to his billing.
He made the occasion especially memorable by
bringing his wife and two teenage daughters.

The restaurant had an interior courtyard filled
with cages of live ducks. We lingered to admire the
handsome birds and I learned they were forcefed
in order to attain a perfection of tenderness and
generous layers of fat just under the skin.

Our dining room was in an upstairs location
overlooking a garden. A table near the windows
held bowls of watermelon seeds. Nearer the en-
trance was a marbletopped table set for the dinner.

We sat around eating watermelon seeds and
chatting over warm rice wine. A waiter brought a
dish of sweet hot walnuts and after that a big
server with slices of smoked salmon, preserved
eggs, sliced ham and pickled duck's livers. There
was a platter of oranges, too, cut in wedges.

A Meal in Three Acts – Act I

An hour passed. The waiter appeared with the
Peking Duck fresh from the oven and splendid on
a bed of lettuce. We admired it and he left, taking
the duck with him. It was time to move to the
dining table.

The waiter returned with a platter. Arranged on
it in fan shape were bite size sections of the duck

skin, crackling crisp on top and succulent with fat underneath. Other platters brought hoisin sauce, a tart thick black sauce, and spring onions cut in two-inch lengths. There was also an array of small steamed white pancakes.

My host showed me what to do — first a pancake, then a thin slice or two of the onion, a piece of duck skin, a spread of the sauce, more onion and finally a second pancake on top.

The thin layer of juicy duck fat and the soft pancakes were perfect opposites for the crunchy skin. The dark sauce was different from any I had ever tasted in China and I doubt it would have pleased me by itself. But added to the crisp skin and rich fat, it was a balanced bouquet of sweets and sours and had a pleasantly gritty texture. As for the onion, I seldom ate them in such quantity but found them right. I thought the pancakes were uncooked, for they were white and flat, but they had been steamed and brushed with sesame oil and tasted of nuts.

What a combination of textures and tastes! What a diversion to be involved in this do-it-yourself service! This involvement added a nice dimension to sharing the meal and I wondered what would happen next.

Peking Duck — Act II, Same Duck

What I had expected first, came second. When we had enjoyed the pancake course, the duck returned, neatly separated from the bones and cut in narrow strips and garnished with coriander greens. There were dishes of vegetables, rice and crusty deepfried fish with sweet-sour sauce.

Peking Duck — Act III, Same Duck

Next came steaming bowls of duck soup made from the duck bones. And after that sweet rice.

And if you were to ask me what we did following dinner, I would reply, Who needs entertainment after a Three-Act Duck Drama in Peking?

You can accomplish the same dramatic parade in the Peking manner with careful prior management.

And this is a version of how it is accomplished.

PEKING DUCK

Reserve four days for this splendid production — three to do justice to the duck and the fourth to receive homage from your friends when you serve it.

Dressing the Duck. Wash and dry, inside and out, a 5 or 6 pound duck. Rub skin and inside with a mixture of 1 teaspoon salt and 2 tablespoons Chinese wine. Store uncovered in refrigerator to dry for two days. Reserve neck for soup.

The third day, glaze the duck with a mixture of 3 tablespoons of honey and equal parts of water. Rub inside and again return uncovered to refrigerator for another day of drying out.

Baking the Duck. Heat oven to 350° and bake duck for 1½ hours. The trick is to hang the duck from the oven rack. This can be accomplished by hanging the bird on metal shower curtain hooks, one on each leg and wing. Place over a pan lined with aluminum foil to catch drippings.

Duck Sauces

Various sauces have been recommended for Peking Duck — plum sauce, soy bean paste sauce and hoisin. Some are served warm and some, cold. So you have a choice.

BEAN PASTE SAUCE

Blend 4 tablespoons soybean paste with 1 tablespoon sesame oil, 1 tablespoon sugar and ¼ cup water. Simmer until thick. Serve warm.

HOISIN SAUCE

Stir 2 tablespoons of sugar into ¼ cup of hoisin sauce and let stand until it is served. Depending on your taste, you can add a small amount of soy sauce and a few drops of sesame oil. Serve cold.

DUCK PANCAKES

The Peking Pancakes I folded over the pieces of duck skin were small, pale and tasty. They are fun to make because you apply bread kneading techniques and the dough is warm and pleasant to work.

Mix well in a heavy bowl (otherwise the sticky dough will pull the bowl around with every turn of the spoon):

1 ¾ cups flour
2/3 cup boiling water poured in gradually

Knead dough until it is smooth and elastic — about 5 minutes and you have a lump the size of a soft ball. Pull it out into a uniform roll about 18 inches long and cut off one-inch pieces.

Dip one piece in sesame oil and press onto an unoiled piece. Roll out both together to make a very thin 4-inch pancake. Fry in oiled wok at moderate heat until bubbles form. Turn and fry other side. Repeat until all dough is used.

As you remove each pancake from wok, pull apart to make two and stack them under a damp towel. When all cakes are ready to serve with duck skin, steam for 10 minutes to reheat.

Peking Duck, Act I is ready for curtain raising. Act II with the slices of roast duck has numerous possible accompaniments — shredded pork with green peppers, fried fish with sweet sour sauce, fried rice or noodles.

The Rest is Duck Soup!

The soup course is the simplest of all. Cook the neck in 3 cups of water with 1 slice of ginger and a green onion. When broth is ready, strain. Add ½ teaspoon each of salt and sugar and ½ head of iceberg lettuce which you have torn into pieces as for a salad or 2 cups Chinese cabbage cut in 1-inch sections. Bring to boil. Soup is ready when greens are still crisp and chewy — about 3 to 5 minutes.

Yield: 6 servings

THE PEKING PANCAKE AND THE ENCOUNTER GROUP

With apologies to Confucius, we modestly offer a Schafer Saying: *The group that eats with its fingers sticks together.*

Joking aside, the participative meal, whatever its nature, has a magic effect on communication and interpersonal exchange.

Many times, the distaff side of the family during teaching days at William Woods College for Women observed this phenomenon in the college dining room. The occasions were the all too rare make-your-own-sandwich luncheons.

Makings of tasty sandwiches were already on the round tables when the girls entered for lunch. They could sit at any table they chose, with any professor. There were hot fresh breads which only a great Southern cook could conjure, crisp greens and assorted fillings. Each helped herself and built a sandwich to her heart's desire.

In an atmosphere of almost childlike gaiety and freedom, an uninhibited flow of talk ensued, marked by openness and earnestness. Eating became a pleasant game, a creative approach to dining, a relaxed sharing. To the sensitive ear, the communication was much more real than when meals took place at assigned tables under assigned

rules for decorum. These participative meals were the only ones my wife recalls with keen pleasure after all the years.

We have seen this same warmth displayed during the experience of eating Peking Pancakes with Peking Duck. The freedom to arrange and select pancake fillings, the novelty, the unexpected informality of getting their hands into play — all contribute to a leveling spirit at the table. What a clever Oriental ploy to make all men brothers at the beginning of a feast! What a good thing to remember when you bring strangers to the table with the hope of making them friends! And what a neat way to make sure you, the host, can also sit down and enjoy the occasion when guests sit down to eat.

Artful Assemblage

The Peking Pancake is a marvelously flexible bread. It receives sauces and solids alike without becoming soaked or unwieldy. It rolls up without breaking or falling apart. It can be handled neatly without spilling. It is the all-purpose wrap.

You can build a whole supper or brunch around it. Just assemble a stack of bigger pancakes and dishes with varied fillings — cold cut meats and hot, scrambled eggs, sea foods, chicken, condiments, sauces and fruit — whatever you fancy will please your guests.

CONFECTIONS - MOON CAKES, JEWELED PUDDING & PEKING DUST

During Japanese occupation of Hong Kong, I gained a hearty appreciation for Chinese sweets. As one of eight volunteers who worked for Dr. Selwyn Clark, director, British Medical Services, I had a pass that permitted me to live in Hong Kong rather than be interned in a prisoner of war camp. I joined a small crew of truck drivers who supplied hospitals with food and fuel and took patients to and from Camp Stanley. We led a Spartan life and lived on very plain food.

With all the brute physical labor, we developed a great craving for sweets. Once, we managed to find and buy a 25-pound chunk of sweet chocolate. We broke it up with a hammer and carried fist size pieces in our pockets to chew on.

Belle Ah Chun, the amah in the big house where we all lived, did the best she could with limited funds and supplies. On one memorable occasion, her husband appeared. A professional cook, he had brought with him a pound of sugar and a half dozen eggs. He generously offered to share them by baking a cake for us.

The austerity of the times faded with the thought of the coming celebration. We sat down to dinner and when it was time for the cake, we waited and waited for the cake to crown the evening.

At last it was not the chef but Belle who appeared with the sweet. It was a cook's disaster. She explained that in an excess of desire to please us, her husband had lavished too much sugar on the cake. Now he had lost much face because the cake had fallen and practically crystallized. Not even a big frosting could have hidden its sorry shape.

But the cake was sweet and that was all we asked. Not a crumb was left. We loved it and tried to convince the cook that by our standards, he was indeed a great cook to make something so toothsome.

It was not lost on me that the gentleman had been magnificent in his gesture: to share his wealth of sugar and eggs in wartime to make a Western-style cake that was never intended to be part of his repertoire.

The Chinese do not, as a rule, end meals with desserts as we do. There is quite enough of sweetness as the meal progresses, lightened with dollops of sugar and honey. Desserts are really superfluous. Chinese dishes have such a balance of sweet and sour, salty and tart that tea is the perfect topping for dinners at home.

Some of the recipes that follow, like the Dragon's Eye Creme, are foreign imports and they rather illustrate what we have so many times observed about our friends of Oriental descent: if you are going to serve a dessert, it had better be the ultimate in luxury. If it's a pie with meringue, make sure the fluff is at least three inches high! If it is a creme, make it exotic! If it is sweet rice, decorate it.

Above all, make it special.

There are, of course, festival sweets like the fruity moon cakes. These appear each October for the Moon Festival just as pumpkin and mince pies appear on our Thanksgiving tables and fruitcakes turn up at Christmastime.

Legend has it that moon cakes were the instrument for smuggling messages to supporters of the famous revolt against tyranny that was prelude to the Ming Dynasty. For old times sake, moon cakes were airlifted last year from Hong Kong to New York especially for Moon Day. Hundreds of people were grateful to buy these imports even at $6.50 each.

You are invited to consider the recipes below for your own private and family celebrations or uprisings.

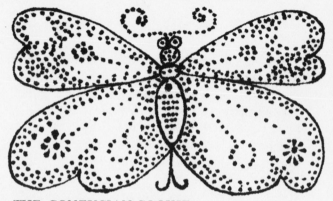

THE CONFUCIAN COOKIE

Let's start with a good old Chinese/American invention, ingeniously born in the Chinese mind but "Made in America" — the Chinese Fortune Cookie. Here is a sweet that joins the pleasure of eating with the Chinese mystique of fortune telling.

Long ago in San Francisco, there was a Fortune Cookie factory just two doors away from where we worked. And if we were willing to forego the delicious excitement of having our fortunes sweetly told, we could buy broken Fortune Cookies for 40¢ a pound. That was enough to supply the office for coffee breaks for several days.

It was more exciting, one day, to be allowed to watch the fantastic cookie machine — complete with middleaged lady cookie-stuffer-bender. We could not see where things began -- all that was behind a screen and mysterious, of course. What we could see was a wondrous conveyor belt with pans at intervals that swung around in a big circle over fixed gas jets.

The cookie lady deftly removed the cookies as they arrived, snapped in a fortune, folded the cookie once and then a second time. In a twinkling, the cookies were cool and ready and generally perfectly shaped.

It was when the cookie bender was not so deft that we profited. And the lady has probably been replaced by a machine in a big factory far away, for Fortune Cookies are rather big business now.

FORTUNE COOKIES

Begin by preparing your messages and fortunes — ingenious, witty, romantic or wise according to the occasion. Type them and have them folded and ready to insert in the warm cookies, for speed is of the essence unless you want to end up with 40¢ a pound seconds!

Now the cookies.

Stir 1-2/3 cups white sugar into 3/4 cup unbeaten egg whites. Salt to taste.
When sugar dissolves, beat in until well blended:

1 cup melted butter
1 cup flour
½ teaspoon vanilla

Drop by teaspoons, well apart, on greased cookie sheet. Bake in 375° oven until edges curl — about 5 minutes. Place messages on cookies, fold cookies over in half once and then mold over a wooden spoon handle. Or on the second folding, stand cookies up in muffin pan cups to cool.

This is hot fast work. If your cookies harden before you have a chance to fold them, return them briefly to the oven to soften. If the folding process is too hot for you to manage quickly with bare hands, wear white cotton gloves.

Recipe yields 60 cookies that have crunch and sweetness far surpassing anything you can buy. And you can save all those egg yolks for Hollandaise sauce or add them to the next day's omelet.

PEKING DUST

This dessert is enough to make an Old China Hand's eyes glaze over. It is said the dust of fabulous Peking is unlike the dust anywhere else. It is dust with a difference and that is why its addition to the name for a dessert honors it.

Peking Dust was introduced in the Northern Chinese city by the Viennese who taught their cooks, who taught everyone else's cook how to cook chestnuts in syrup and build them up into a mound to look like etherealized dust.

They say you can do all kinds of magic with sugar in Peking because the air is so dry — something to remember that day you make Peking Dust. Something else to remember is that Peking Dust is only for chestnut lovers. The dish requires all too much effort to be served to the indifferent. And you might as well be put on notice that purists claim no chestnuts in America are as good as those roasted in sand in China. On the other hand, you can rejoice that chestnuts are less caloric and contain more vitamin C than other nuts.

First prepare 1 cup of pecans according to the recipe for *Walnut and Cashew Nougats* and set aside to decorate your Peking Dust like a necklace.

½ pound chestnuts
1 cup brown sugar
1 teaspoon vanilla
2 tablespoons rum
1 cup water

3 cups whipping cream
3 tablespoons white sugar

Roast, shell and blanch chestnuts. Simmer until tender in a little of the brown sugar and water in a heavy covered kettle. Cool and puree nuts in a blender. Boil remaining sugar, water with rum and vanilla and add to chestnut puree.

Whip cream until it forms stiff peaks. Add sugar. Form a cone shape with the whipped cream on a chilled dish. Carefully cover the cone with the chestnut puree until it is completely masked. Arrange the necklace of pecans around the base, display and prepare to serve at once.

If this operation is too nerve wracking, you can dismiss the theatrics and simply fold the pureed chestnuts into the sweetened whipping cream and freeze until set. This makes a good *Chestnut Ice* that is just as Viennese as Peking Dust.

When we created a Peking Dust Sundae with pureed rum flavored chestnuts and chopped pecans as a topper for vanilla icecream, our favorite film connoisseur rated it *scrumdillyumptious.*

EIGHT PRECIOUS FRUITS PUDDING

Here is a dish that is very dear to an old friend if we are to judge by the soft look on her face when she described it, and if we place value on the fact that it came first to her mind.

Like *Riz à l'Imperatrice,* the French classic, this rice dish is molded, though the Chinese process is different. And the fruity embellishment of the Chinese dish is the more formal of the two.

A delight for children to anticipate, this dish suggests a good "busy work" project for a cold, winter day. Have the small ones make the design. Let them have some freewheeling fun, even if their efforts end with a puckish face instead of a formal flower-and-leaf design in the bottom of the bowl.

1 cup glutinous rice
½ cup brown sugar or honey
2 tablespoons shortening
Handful of chopped dried persimmons, dates, raisins and lichee nuts

Cook rice. When it cools a little add sugar, shortening and chopped fruits. Mix well.

Assemble assorted fruits and nuts to make a design and cut into strips and other desired shapes:

Green plum
Cherry
Lotus seeds
Dates
Chestnuts, walnuts and almonds
Other fresh or glace fruit as desired

Butter a mold or bowl and arrange fruit and nuts in a pattern in the bottom. Spoon prepared rice into mold without disturbing the design. Place mold on a rack in your wok, cover and steam for an hour.

Unmold while rice is still hot. Present it whole on a dish for your guests to admire the art and prepare to serve at once with a sauce made from 1/3 cup sugar and 1 cup water, thickened with corn starch and flavored with almond extract.

The Ubiquitous Almond

Fortune Cookies popularly end meals for tourists in Chinatown. They have appeared as novelties at cocktail parties with numbers inside to direct guests to appointed tables. Occasionally a giant one is the receptacle of a prize.

The cookie we have more often enjoyed at the end of a Chinese meal is made with almonds.

ALMOND COOKIES

These are very crisp and rich, very easy to make. Stored in a tight tin, they have excellent keeping qualities.

1 cup lard
1 cup sugar
2 eggs — one for the dough, the other for brushing on top
1 teaspoon almond flavoring
2½ cups flour sifted with ¼ teaspoon soda
36 almonds, halved

Lightly roast almond halves and set aside.

Beat lard and sugar together until light. Add one egg and almond flavoring, mixing thoroughly. Add flour mix gradually. This will make a velvety dough.

Roll walnut-size balls of dough with your hands. Press balls flat on ungreased cookie sheet. Beat second egg and with pastry brush apply to each cookie before pressing an almond into the center.

Bake in slow oven at 300° for 20 minutes. Increase heat to 350° and continue baking 10 minutes. Remove cookies carefully and cool on a rack. Yield: 6 dozen

This uncomplicated recipe lends itself to experimentation and variation.

Sprinkle toasted sesame seeds on top before baking or add ½ cup to dough during mixing.

Dip end of a chopstick into food coloring and make a happy indentation. Decorate with pine nuts. It's all up to you.

MOON CAKES

To own a hand carved moon cake mold is novel enough, but to own one that is used is very special indeed. Beautiful decorations in any kitchen, they deserve to be labeled art objects. They have the shape of big food scoops and are hewn of solid hardwood into which is carved a small round well, three inches in diameter and half again as deep. The bottom of the well is variously carved with dragons, phoenixes, ideographs or abstract flower forms. This bottom becomes the top of the cake.

We borrowed one that had a cracked handle, made whole again with a big bolt and screw. We soon learned why the crack developed.

The well shapes and decorates the cakes. Sometimes they have a whole pigeon egg inside. Sometimes they are glorified fruitcakes with a pastry coat as they are in the recipe that follows.

First prepare a pastry crust with

2 level cups of sifted, all-purpose flour
¾ cup lard
½ teaspoon salt
3 level tablespoons ice water

Cut flour and shortening in a bowl with a blending fork. Add water, 1 tablespoon at a time, until flour and shortening form a smooth ball. Cut dough into balls and let rest.

Prepare a filling. Into a paste made with 1/3 cup sugar, 1 tablespoon shortening, 2 tablespoons rice flour and 2 tablespoons water, stir 2 tablespoons each:

Raisins, pine nuts, toasted sesame seeds and finely chopped peanuts and chestnuts.
Candied fruits according to your preference.

Roll out pastry balls to make thin skins to line well of moon cake mold. Fill with nut and fruit mix and top opening of mold with a pastry cover, pinching cover down to mold lining so there are no holes.

Release finished moon cake by whacking the mold down forcefully on a folded towel on a bread board. You'll now understand why a moon cake mold can crack!

Repeat lining and filling operation until you have used all ingredients. Place moon cakes on a buttered cookie sheet and brush with a mixture of beaten egg yolk and 1 teaspoon sesame oil to give them a lacquered look. Bake in a slow oven 250° for 20 to 30 minutes.

These are so rich that we serve them in slivers, just as we serve Christmas fruitcake.

Don't despair if you have no moon cake mold. Simply bake your moon cakes in muffin tins. They might be small, but you can still press designs into topping dough with a cookie press and slip in a message if you feel like a Secret Agent.

T'ANG HU LU'RH – CANDIED FRUITS

Every child knows that some sweets should come on a nibbling stick and be free of grownup restraints of etiquette and dishware. But don't expect children in your family to keep these sweets in their innocent province. Grownups like them, too.

This recipe, unrevised, is from the yellowed pages of the Peking cookbook.

Red fruit, grapes, sections of orange, walnuts or other fruits are pierced by a wooden skewer about 8 inches long. The fruit and nuts are so arranged that different varieties alternate and that about half the stick is covered with fruit and the other half serves as a handle. The fruit is then dipped in syrup and put in a cold place. (This can be prepared in cold weather only.)

The syrup is made by boiling 2½ pounds of sugar and 2 cups of water till it makes a very brittle ball when dropped in cold water.

With refrigerators so common these days, you won't have to be like the Peking ladies and wait for

cold weather to make candies on a stick. Also you can add any fruits and nuts that are available and skewerable — pitted cherries, sections of pears, peaches, plums, pineapples and oranges, figs, dates, chestnuts and seedless grapes. Ask the children to make suggestions. And if you are using canned

fruits, use the fruit juice to make the syrup.

It would be very sensible to explain to the small ones that skewers are not playthings. Encourage them to return sticks to you for seconds to be made some other time.

TOFFEE APPLES

The Chinese frankly admit that American apples are superior to their own. For whatever reason, they give this fruit fancy dress. Here is a recipe that takes you back to the wok.

1 tablespoon toasted sesame seeds
3 tablespoons flour
1 tablespoon cornstarch
1 egg white
2/3 cup water
3 firm fleshed apples
Salad oil for deep frying

Mix flour, cornstarch, egg white and water in a bowl. Peel and core apples, removing any imperfections and slicing into six wedges.

Dip wedges into flour mix, coating thoroughly. Deepfry in wok until just golden but not mushy. Drain on paper toweling.

Prepare syrup with

2/3 cup brown sugar
1/3 cup water
1/4 cup light syrup

CARMELED BANANAS

Carmeled Bananas are prepared much the same as Toffee Apples, except for the light batter and deep frying.

Peel firm bananas and cut into quarters. Fry in light oil in the wok until brown.

Prepare a dipping syrup in a sauce pan over direct heat with:

1 cup brown sugar
1/3 cup corn syrup
1/4 teaspoon salt
1/3 cup water

Cook quickly over direct heat without stirring. When syrup is almost to carmel stage, plunge pot into ice water to stop cooking process. Then place pot in pan of hot water to keep syrup fluid.

Dip fried apple slices in syrup, sprinkle with sesame and dip into ice water. If you serve wedges on tin, they won't stick. Otherwise, serve on lightly buttered dishes.   Yield: 6 servings

Completely coat sections of banana with hot syrup, dash in ice water and serve on your finest Mexican tin sprinkled with chopped roasted nuts, grated lemon rind or candied ginger.

SCHOLAR'S BOOK SHELF

Food and friendship appear to be inseparable to the Chinese. Food preoccupied kings and philosophers alike. Confucius made pronouncements about its art. China had its own Brillat-Savarin in 18th Century Yuan Mei.

To search out secrets of Chinese cookery requires a tireless, resourceful and energetic investigation of sources. You find yourself in conversation with many people in many communities. Every visit to a new library or new bookstore yields surprises. Each has its individual list and selection because each has a different buyer and a different public.

Among our friends are many Old China Hands. The Boone sisters, Muriel and Frances, whose family members were known as missionaries in China as early as 1835, generously talked about Chinese cuisine with us in Santa Fe for two days. Then they sent us off with long out-of-print cookbooks that originated in Peking and Okinawa.

Sometimes a find comes to light because of sheer

instinct and pure doggedness in pursuing questions. Stockton, California, we thought, just had to have something extra in the way of Chinese cook books.

So we went to the public library there and found an interesting "Ethnic Culture" listing which included "Chinese Ancestry." We found six cook books listed. In discussing this list with a Chinese librarian, we mentioned how often we had heard of YWCA's and church groups that sponsored classes in Chinese cuisine.

"Oh," exclaimed the young lady. "You should talk to my aunt downstairs in the newspaper section. She belongs to the Women's Society of Christian Service at St. Mark's Methodist Church. I know she contributed recipes to their cook book."

So we met Mrs. Thelma Yim and came to possess a very interesting cook book with 217 pages of Chinese recipes

"humbly presented with the hope that you will

93

NOTES & COMMENTS

enjoy the Cantonese dishes that we use daily in our homes and on special festive occasions. We further hope that the next generation will find the recipes helpful as they establish their homes and try to 'cook as mother and grandmother did.'"

The book was edited by Mrs. Thomas C. Wong and came out in December, 1966 — something we would never have discovered if we hadn't persisted with our questions. We cannot understand why this cook book wasn't included in the library list in Stockton!

Cooking Schools

A special resource in large communities is the presence of cooking schools, some privately managed for coteries and others open to public enrollment in limited numbers for a reasonable fee. The latter are often part of YWCA curricula and taught by well-known chefs.

It is wise, however, to inquire what such courses offer before enrolling. One of our friends, herself a Chinese — discovered that her cooking teacher spoke a dialect she didn't understand. The teacher relied on an interpreter and compounded frustrations by giving out no copies of recipes.

Book Notes

The 20 books we have listed represent a wide range from amateur to professional, from simple to elaborate, from inexpensive to lavish. Each one deserves a reading. Many deserve translation to your kitchen.

Some are out of print and worth the effort to get your favorite bookseller to institute a search. Most of them are in public libraries of any size at all and you can borrow and sample before you buy.

You will, of course, run across many more books than we have described — in print, out of print and privately published. The field is growing. Good hunting!

Chang, Isabelle C., *Chinese Cooking Made Easy,* Paperback Library, Coronet Communications, Inc., New York, 7th printing, 1970. Mrs. Chang's book is a sharing of "how nutritious, low in calories, inexpensive and simple Chinese cooking can be" as well as how varied and historically interesting. Several times an author of Chinese cook books, she has arranged this book by festivals and seasons for "healthful and economical reasons." The book is also organized according to the days of the week: Sunday, poultry day; Monday, pork day, etc. This may strike you as trite, but the folk tales and stories sprinkled throughout the text and the variety of dishes — nearly 400 — make this a worthwhile addition to your cook book shelf for only $.75. A good index restores order to a book otherwise fragmented by its concept.

Chao, Buwei Yang, *How to Cook and Eat in Chinese,* John Day Co., New York, 1945. This was the first book on Chinese cookery in our library and for many years the only one. It was reprinted last year by Random and sells for $6.95.

In Canada, we found a paperback version of the book brought out in 1968 by Faber and Faber Ltd., London. It cost $2.10 and brought us up to date on the folksy doctor with the frying pans. She has added chapters of great interest to dieters.

In its way, this book represents a fantastic achievement. A medical doctor, Dr. Chao, like many of the graduate students we knew in college, learned to cook out of desperation. Her distinguished introducers — Ambassador to the United States Hu Shih and author and humanitarian Pearl Buck — were warm in their praise.

"How did I learn to cook so many things?" she asked. "My answer is: with an open mind and an open mouth. I grew up with the idea that nice ladies should not be in a kitchen, but, as I told you, necessity opened my mind first. Then being often left to my own devices under all sorts of conditions has made me feel most conventions of cooking, serving, and eating to be a little silly. It is well to know the exact practice in China, in America, and in dietetics, but nothing takes the place of a little thinking. If you cannot get beef, get pork. If you cannot find an eggbeater, use your head."

By her "open mouth," she meant she asked questions wherever she traveled in her own country. She was not ashamed to ask how this dish or that pastry was prepared and where the materials came from.

It was her claim that if she had eaten anything, she could cook it if you gave her long enough time to try.

"Since I know what it ought to taste like, I can be my own judge as to whether I am getting nearer or farther from the right taste after each try, and that's the way to learn."

Dr. Chao was responsible for many terms, like stirfry, now accepted by all of us who cook in Chinese. Her descriptions of methods and materials and her recipes are excellent, although we always found her numbering system too Dewey-Decimaled for our tastes.

But the treasury of facts, techniques, and Chinese lore dished up with a wonderful sense of humor and sometimes waggishly footnoted by her husband still keeps this book at the head of our Chinese library.

Dr. Chao closes with a Table of Recipes in Chinese and English with those confounded recipe numbers. Her index is excellent.

Chen, Joyce, *Joyce Chen Cook Book*, J.B. Lippincott Co., Philadelphia, 1962, $6.95. In its 9th printing, this book is doubtless popular because of the eminently practical advice of the author who is also a Chinese restaurateur, teacher and TV personality. Especially good are her shopping tips and counsel on what to buy in foods, and what you will encounter as a cook. She even has a shopping list at the end of her book which you can tear out and use. It lists Chinese and English names for foods with such helpful remarks as "Hoi Sin Sauce in square or round cans. Round is easier to open."

Type is large and easy to read. Recipes are simple to follow. Drawings show step-by-step methods for folding egg rolls, using chop sticks, preparing chicken, wrapping Peking Duck, and making noodles and won ton skins.

Joyce Chen is deeply concerned that her book satisfy your needs both as a cook and as a shopper. She invites correspondence from those who want more help with cooking and shopping. An excellent buy.

Chu, Grace Zia, *The Pleasures of Chinese Cooking,* Cornerstone Library, New York, 1970. Distributed by Simon & Schuster, $1.45 Mrs. Chu groups recipes for full-course, balanced meals for four persons or banquet dishes for eight. Craig Claiborne, retired food editor of the New York *Times,* claims Mrs. Chu "is pos-

sessed of the magic involved in using the wok, the traditional cooking utensil, to the greater glory of the human palate."

All recipes show time required for preparation and cooking. With this information, you can start first with dishes that take the longest time to prepare and cook. Recipes close with enlightening paragraphs of tips on ingredients, alternatives, substitutions and cautions.

She has practical and helpful introductory chapters on the ingredients of Chinese cooking; cutting with the Chinese cleaver; working with woks and chop sticks; cooking methods; tea; the right way to order food in a Chinese restaurant; growing bean sprouts in your kitchen; a list of stores in New York City, Boston, Chicago, Los Angeles, San Francisco and Washington, D.C., that sell Chinese foods and other ingredients.

Mrs. Chu's style is easy. Her commendable aim seems to be to make you comfortable with Chinese customs as well as with your role as a Chinese cook. An excellent buy.

Feng, Doreen Yen Hung, *The Joy of Chinese Cooking,* Grosset & Dunlap, New York, $3.95. One of a series of books under the title of "Expert's Choice Cook Books," this book is also illustrated by the author. She sets out to bring joy, excitement and a little bit of China into your kitchen, home and life. In many, many ways, this is a beautiful book, presented with style and humor. There is, indeed, joy in her cooking. Another good buy.

Froud, Nina, *Cooking the Chinese Way,* Spring Books, London, 1960. Reprinted in 1963. One of a series on cooking around the world, this is the work of a bustling, busy, no-nonsense cook who has a nice feeling for enjoying her own cooking. This seems to us to be a vital life sign for any cook.

Nina Froud advises forthrightly, shares food experiences from her life in China and suggests what are "musts" in the Chinese kitchen in such a way as to win quick compliance on your part. You know she knows what she is talking about when she tells you about foods, methods and customs.

A second title for this book might be "Cooking the Chinese Way Without Fear!" Excellent range of Cantonese recipes, all indexed. Weights and measures are English but book has conversion tables for American readers. Look for this book in your library because it seems to be out of print.

Hahn, Emily, *The Cooking of China,* Time-Life Books, New York, 1968, $7.95. From the "Foods of the World Series", this book fits a standard: 208 pages, 8½x11 format, 40,000 words, lavish color photography, and step-by-step pictures of cooking methods. Hundreds of thoroughly tested recipes are explained in detail. Because it is such a coffee table extravaganza, the editors have cleverly accompanied it with a separate spiral bound recipe booklet on which you can spill and spatter to your heart's content.

As an Old China Hand, I can say this book, compared with many others I have seen, represents the ultimate for those desiring to saturate themselves in the environment, sophistication and professional techniques of Chinese cuisine. Impressive as well as useful, the book is a great value. Read it and look at it for the sheer pleasure of it and cook with its recipe supplement to your greater glory.

Hong, Wallace Yee, *Chinese Cook Book,* Crown Publishers, Inc., New York, 1952, $3.95. This is a man's idea of a cook book. Every recipe is numbered, named in English and Chinese and then actually outlined from A to Z.

It is significant that this is the only library cook book I ran into that was liberally decorated with signs of cooking battles — spotted with drops of soy here and there, and smudged and thumbed with oil! It was well used!

You may smile over the A,B,C arrangement of recipe directions at your elbow, but stick with the method at the start and you will learn to dispense with these constraints soon enough.

Good recipes in a wide range; good practical information; good suggestions make this book worth looking for, spots and all.

Hong Kong and China Gas Co., Ltd., *Towngas Cookery Book,* $5.95. This big book was designed, printed and published in Hong Kong using local talent for collecting, testing and translating international recipes. The span of its influence is indicated by the fact that it was proudly lent to us as a useful tool by both an American missionary who grew up and worked for years in China and a Chinese homemaker who came to America many years ago as a picture bride. The 1970 edition has 397 pages.

The book was first published to celebrate the gas company's centennial and nine editions followed in response to demand. Reflecting the international tastes of Hong Kong residents, the book offers typical recipes from 16 countries from assorted cold foods to toffee apples.

The Chinese section includes 60 recipes. All recipes are printed in English and Chinese and lavishly illustrated in color and in black and white photographs. Recipes and methods of preparation are geared to the housewife, not the professional. Instructions include many local terms — as 1 catty lean pork, a catty being the Chinese measure for about 1-1/3 pounds. There is a good index of recipes by title.

Kan, Johnny and Charles Leong, *Eight Immortal Flavors*, Howell-North Books, Berkeley, California, 1963, $5.95.

This book is by the innovator who spearheaded the movement to educate non-Orientals and American-born Chinese in the art of the wok and other Chinese kitchen utensils by setting up a hotel-type dining room with a glassed-in kitchen. He it was who instituted the first delivery service for Chinese food and progressed from education in Chinese cuisine to introducing more complicated Cantonese dishes in an elegant and dignified atmosphere.

Mr. Kan has a connoisseur's approach to both the art of cooking and the methods. He is obviously one of the most experienced restaurateurs in the business and deserves a wide audience.

Lamb, Corrine, *The Chinese Festive Board*, Frederick A. Stokes Co., New York, 1936. Alas, this book is no longer in print.

If it is true that you have to be half detective, half adventurer and a little mad to be a perfect Chinese cook, Corrine Lamb will merrily provide you with methods and reasons for arriving at this interesting condition. She is serious about the business, but a delicious informality warmed by an obvious love of things and foods Chinese makes her book a romp.

If it is not possible to buy a copy secondhand, storm the doors of your nearest big library and ask the librarian to hunt down this book for you. Excellent recipes, an English-Chinese dictionary of foodstuffs, useful advice on practically everything!

Lee, Calvin, *Chinese Cooking for American Kitchens,* G.P. Putnam's Sons, New York, 1959. This, too, is no longer in print.

Mr. Lee takes you on a tour of a Chinese kitchen to put you at ease with the equipment and utensils. In the process, he is able to describe their special properties and uses, give them Chinese names and in general prepare you for the correct state of mind in preparing and cooking Chinese foods; in timing the operation; and in the etiquette of serving and dining.

He is an organizer who will give you the best reasons for starting your Chinese dinner with a clean kitchen. We heartily concur! Check this book out of your library if you like exposition as a preface to action. Charmingly illustrated.

Lee, Gary, *The Wok,* Pacific Productions, 1970, $3.95.

This is a beginner's book which takes Chinese cookery very seriously. Beautifully illustrated by Mike Nelson, the book suffers somewhat from the acerbic, sometimes negative ego of the writer. If you can overcome that shading of spirit, you will find the book both helpful and useful. Indexed. About 80 recipes, in a wide range, using the wok, of course, and other utensils.

Lee, Jim, *Jim Lee's Chinese Cookbook,* Harper & Row, New York, 1968, $8.95. Jim Lee's purpose is to teach how to cook the Chinese way, not just to hand you a parcel of recipes. He breaks Chinese cooking down to logical sequences of simple steps and includes tips on substitutions and variations possible with his dishes. His suggestions and explanations are sensible. The book includes essentials of Chinese cooking, planning a Chinese meal, stocking a Chinese larder, storing food, and organizing your cooking operation. Well illustrated. An excellent buy.

Lee, Su Jan, *The Fine Art of Chinese Cooking*, Gramercy Publishing Co., New York, 1962. Now out of print. Dr. Lee's expressed goal is to help you be an inspired and intelligent Chinese chef. He stresses the environmental aspects of the perfect meal — the dining area, the color and quality of dishes, the arrangement of the table, the very names of the dishes.

"One can delight in the vision, logic, surprise, wit and subtlety which distinguishes a really inspired dish from a merely competent one."

A scholar in action, a poet in feeling and a gourmet in spirit, he is also practical. He sees the nutritional trends in the healthful Chinese diet. He thinks of a meal as a symphonic composition of tastes, colors and textures. He thinks of the cook as a scientist using the kitchen as a laboratory for culinary excellence.

In a word, Dr. Lee makes you feel you are about to enter a delightful career without having to equip yourself with more than a wok, a pair of chop stocks and a good sharp cleaver. And he is urbane enough to say that the American invention, chop suey, should not be banished; it should be improved and he tells you how!

He gives recipes and instructions for traditional Chinese food; Chinese foods with an American touch; and American food with a Chinese touch. And, bully for him, he isn't above telling you how to use leftovers. There is a good index but in such dreadfully small type it's difficult to read. Try to find this book in the library. You'll enjoy Dr. Lee.

Lin, Tsuifeng and Hsiangju, *Secrets of Chinese Cooking*, Prentice-Hall, Inc., Englewood Cliffs, N.J., 1960, $4.95. With an essay on "The Art of Cooking and Dining in Chinese" by Lin Yutang. This book has appeared with various titles — a fact which confused us. But there is no doubt it exalts Chinese cooking as a fine art, offering both the why of methods and the how-to.

To use this book is to have a dignified kitchen guide that is literate and amiable. As a gourmet cook, you will be saying as you read, "Now, there's something I wanted to know" or "What decorum!" or "What a gracious way to reveal cooking secrets!" or "What thoughtful, keenly observant practitioners!" So this is a must for milady's Chinese/American kitchen. There is no coy reluctance to share secrets.

Our one complaint is that we like to see recipes with the whole list of ingredients before we go to work with them. This is a big help with shopping, which, after all, is the first task of the cook.

A good index. An excellent buy for many of the same reasons you will want Grace Chu's book.

Ma, Nancy Chih, *Mrs. Ma's Favorite Chinese Recipes,* Kodansha International Ltd., Tokyo and Palo Alto, California, 1968, $5.95. Mrs. Ma's hypothesis is that the Chinese present one of the world's most delicious, easy-to-prepare, and economical cuisines. The authenticity of 25 full-color and 150 black-and-white photographs presenting utensils, food preparation, cooking methods and finished dishes on the table are convincing proof of the beauty and appeal of Chinese cuisine. They also help the neophyte identify foods and dishes correctly.

The Table of Contents includes basics of cooking and recipes divided according to seasons of the year. Special sections take up rice, dumplings and noodles; desserts; wine, tea and table service.

Mrs. Ma claims to offer 150 completely new fool-proof recipes. This is her eighth cook book. There is a glossary of English/Chinese terms for beverages, cooking methods, cutting methods, fish and crustaceans, fruit and nuts, meat and poultry, rice, noodles and dumplings, seasonings and sauces and finally vegetables.

A good index. This is a well-illustrated tool from the hands of the lady who, among other things, taught the Imperial Princesses of Japan how to cook.

Miller, Gloria Bley, *The Thousand Recipe Chinese Cookbook,* Grosset and Dunlap, New York, 1970, $10. An elegant, 927-page book that lifts you — if you can lift it! — into the class of wealthy scholars. The drawings by Earl Thollander are captivatingly beautiful and decorate practically every page.

Mrs. Miller lists 294 ingredients used in Chinese cooking and describes some in detail in her glossary of terms.

Comprehensive and authoritative, the book is the winner of the Tastemaker Award for excellence and is the basic handbook for the who, what, where, and how of Chinese cooking. The number and variations of recipes are somewhat bewildering in sheer volume. Don't expect to simply read a recipe. The author will send you flying all over her book with her cross references.

Sunset, *Oriental Cook Book,* Lane Books, Menlo Park, California. Chopstick cookery for Beginners in Chinese, Japanese and Korean Cuisine. 3rd printing, January, 1971, $1.95. Here is a beautiful paperback illustrated with both drawings and photographs. *Sunset* Magazine editors and the *Sunset* test kitchen have brought their famous technical excellence to the essence of Oriental cuisine; ingredient shopping guide; tools and utensils and how to use them; meal planning; and recipes. Good readable index. A fine buy.

Wong, Evelyn, ed., *Treasured Recipes from Two Cultures — American and Chinese,* Women's Society of Christian Service, St. Mark's United Methodist Church, Stockton, California, $4.50 plus small handling charge. This good little spiral bound book had gone through three printings — 1966, 1967, 1969. The recipes are contributions from church members and friends or attributed to the editor.

The foreword warns:

"No substitutions have been made — this is the way we cook! Where known, English names are used for ingredients. Otherwise, Cantonese pronunciations are used. Good Chinese chefs cook from memory with *no* measurements, thermometers, or timing. Those in our recipes are approximate to serve as a guide. Practice makes perfect. You will learn to adjust to quantity and your family's taste."

This is not a slick book that promises to make you an instant success. The ladies of St. Mark's are depending on you to *think* while you cook in Chinese and to dare to be adventurous. The implication is that of course you will have times that will try your soul, but don't despair.

In the meantime, you can feel sure you are getting plainspoken advice from those who want to share treasured recipes from their ancient culture. Although they pride themselves on being Chinese, the ladies do make practical concessions to their American kitchens, grocery shelves, too, and provide useful tips on shortcuts and packaged foods. A good buy for your kitchen book shelf.

INDEX

The Wokcraft index is more than an index — It is a reference as well as a dictionary and pronunciation guide for key words you might need while shopping. The pronunciations are in the Cantonese dialect most widely used by Chinese grocers in the U.S.

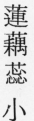

OTHER BOOKS BY CHARLES & VIOLET SCHAFER

PUBLISHED BY TAYLOR & NG

HERBCRAFT

EGGCRAFT

BREADCRAFT

TEACRAFT

COFFEE